About the Author

Delyth Swann has worked with children all her life and is passionate about encouraging more families to explore our beautiful countryside. She trained as a paediatric nurse at Great Ormond Street Hospital. Years later, after moving to Minehead with her husband and three children, she worked in the local first school supporting children in English and Maths.

Delyth shared the secret of trig points with her two young daughters 27 years ago, as they were walking in the Yorkshire Dales. Since then, the family have spent many holidays walking amongst hills and mountains. To this day, Katie, Nicki and Jamie are still intrigued to know the stories behind the trig points they visit.

Tales from The Trig Points
The Discovery

Delyth Swann

Tales from The Trig Points
The Discovery

Olympia Publishers
London

www.olympiapublishers.com
OLYMPIA PAPERBACK EDITION

A CIP catalogue record for this title is
available from the British Library.

ISBN: 978-1-78830-298-2

This is a work of fiction.
Names, characters, places and incidents originate from the writer's
imagination. Any resemblance to actual persons, living or dead, is purely
coincidental.

First Published in 2020

Olympia Publishers
Tallis House
2 Tallis Street
London
EC4Y 0AB

Printed in Great Britain

Dedication

To my beautiful children, Katie, Nicki and Jamie, who inspired me to write this book and to my husband, Nick, whose endless love and support is truly amazing.

Acknowledgements

I would like to thank my husband, Nick, for proofreading, but most of all for his constant support and belief in me. Also, thank you to my children, Katie, Nicki and Jamie, for reading the drafts and for all their encouragement.

Finally, I would like to thank everyone at Olympia Publishers, who made it possible for my dream to come true.

Introduction

Thousands of people all over the world have walked to trig points on top of hills and mountains and never given a thought as to the purpose they serve, other than to mark a point of reference on an Ordnance Survey Map. Many are now being demolished as satellites are used in their place. The following story sheds light onto a far more important reason for their existence. It not only exposes the vulnerability of the Trignomes who live within them, but could help to ensure their very survival.

Chapter One

The path ahead was rocky and steeper than Jonathan had imagined. He carefully picked his way over the uneven ground. The climb was hard and his heart was racing. Jonathan shone his torch along the path and although he was concerned the battery might run out, he needed the light from time to time, as he didn't want to risk spraining his ankle. Fortunately there was a full moon, which allowed him moments when he could see the path quite clearly. It gradually became slightly less rocky, but even steeper, as he got closer to the top. He had to keep stopping to catch his breath. At last he was able to climb up the last few steps carved into the stone and reach the summit.

There it was; the majestic white cross rose before him. Jonathan didn't really know what he had expected to find or feel at this moment, but the magical solutions to his problems did not seem to be flooding into his mind as he had hoped. He circled the cross, looking at it from all angles. It towered above him and he had to really strain his neck to look up towards the top. As the moon shone down it somehow reflected off the cross, making it almost gleam. He clung to it tightly and cried out in desperation.

'Please help me. Please, please, please,' he sobbed.

The night air was chilling and Jonathan was beginning to cool off rapidly now he had stopped walking. He hadn't thought beyond this point in his plans. He'd just expected everything to fall into place and he would know what to do. But the problem was, he didn't. He looked around and suddenly felt exhausted. The lack of sleep, the brisk walk, along with the nervous energy he'd burned up, had all combined to make him feel utterly drained. All he wanted to do was curl up and sleep. He took out the blanket he had remembered to pack at the last minute and tried to snuggle up at the base of the cross. The stony ground underneath didn't seem to bother him. He couldn't think straight anymore. He thought about his cosy bed at home and wished he were there. Wrapping the blanket tightly around him, he buried his face inside and closed his eyes. Within moments Jonathan was asleep.

He had no idea how long he'd slept for. He seemed to sleep in fits and starts, waking with a shiver, his feet feeling numb inside his trainers. He ate some chicken and a couple of roast potatoes. It was hard to hold them with his frozen hands and getting the food into his mouth was even harder as he was shivering so much. If only he had thought to bring a flask of hot milk, but nine-year-old boys can't think of everything! He finished off with a banana, hoping that this would give him the energy he needed. Feeling a little revitalised, and with the sun beginning to rise, he knew he should move. However, standing proved much more difficult than he could have possibly imagined. His feet were completely numb, causing him to fall over as soon as he tried to put weight on them. He slumped back down and tried to think what to do, but as he was so cold and trembling uncontrollably, it was almost impossible. He suddenly remembered Mrs Milson standing outside church one Sunday, banging one foot against the other and jumping up and down when she thought no one was looking. The heating had broken down in the church and it had been bitterly cold during the service. Mrs Milson had seen Jonathan looking at her with a questioning and perplexed look on his face.

'Don't worry child,' she said smiling. 'I'm all right; it's just a good way of getting the circulation back into my toes. It was so cold inside and sitting still for all that time, well I just can't feel my feet.'

He knew then that's what he had to do. He stood up slowly, this time holding onto the cross for support. He banged his feet together hard, but nothing seemed to be happening. Jumping up and down was even trickier but he persevered. Gradually he could feel some tingling in his feet, and then a sharp pain that made him want to cry out. After what seemed like an eternity he felt much warmer all over and he could take a few steps without losing his balance. He packed his blanket back in his rucksack and started to make his way down the way he had come the night before.

'But where am I going?' Jonathan said to himself in despair. 'Has all this been for nothing?' A sense of bewilderment and insecurity overcame him and he stopped in his tracks and looked back towards the cross.

'Why haven't you helped me?' he yelled. He looked down the steep track that lay in front of him. He had no choice; he had to head back down. It was even harder than climbing up. Some of the rocks were shiny from the constant passage of people going up and down the hill and were quite slippery. Not realising this, Jonathan fell back and landed hard on the stony ground. It took him completely by surprise, but something inside him made him get straight up and this time he placed his feet more carefully as he made his way down. When he reached the gate at the bottom he hesitated. He looked along the path that would take him towards the car park and Ilam beyond. He wasn't ready to go back yet; he knew that for sure. He still had plenty of food supplies, enough for another day at least and Mrs Milson wasn't expecting him back until Wednesday. With a meaningful stride he stepped through the gate on his right and headed north. The path soon led away from the river and he climbed the wide stone steps to the top of Lover's Leap.

Jonathan stopped and looked around him. It was much lighter now, and although the sun had not long started to rise, the light gave an almost mystical feel to the limestone cliff. He remembered the story Joe the gardener had told him about how Lover's Leap had got its name. He'd said that a young girl had climbed the steps and thrown herself off the precipice as she was heartbroken. Luckily, the bushes broke her fall and saved her from being killed. Jonathan tentatively looked over the edge of the stone pile. He thought of the young girl and wondered how desperate she must have been feeling. He sat down and precariously dangled his legs over the side. He thought about his own mother. Where was she now? If only he knew why she had abandoned him. He had asked Mrs Milson once, a couple of years ago. She said the police had done everything they could to try and find her. They had thought that she had probably been very young and maybe just couldn't manage on her own. Mrs Milson said his mother must have loved him very much to give him up so he could have a better life. He had never understood that. How could he have a better life without his real mum?

A strange noise seemed to be coming from nearby, distracting Jonathan's gloomy thoughts. He looked around and could just make out something squirming underneath a craggy rock. He got up and cautiously went to investigate. As he bent down to get a closer look he jumped back in surprise. Half trapped by the rock was what looked vaguely like one of those gnomes he'd seen in people's gardens. However, this one was very different; he was alive for a start and his features were wrinkly, with spikey hair protruding from all over his face and a white beard that reached down to below his waist. He was just a bit taller than the length of Jonathan's hand. His black eyes bulged out of his head, their size almost too big to fit with his small face. He glared out at Jonathan with a mixture of terror and anger. The tail of his long brown coat was trapped so tightly under the rock he'd been unable to wriggle free.

'Don't just stand there,' he screeched at Jonathan. 'Can't you see I need help? I'm not lying by this rock for fun you know.'

'Oh sorry,' Jonathan replied rather nervously. He carefully rolled the rock away and the little gnome stood up briskly, brushing himself down with his hands as he did so.

'Thank you,' the gnome nodded to Jonathan and appeared a little calmer in his manner.

They both stood motionless, staring at each other, not quite knowing what to do next. Jonathan knelt down and began to speak as steadily as he could. However, his voice sounded a little shaky, as he was unable to completely disguise the uncertainty he felt inside.

'My name's Jonathan,' he said softly. 'What's yours?'

The little gnome seemed to be frozen to the spot. After the initial show of bravado, he now appeared to have completely lost his voice and was looking distinctly edgy. Jonathan tried to reassure him with a smile.

As Freddy looked up at Jonathan he found himself almost drawn into his soft blue eyes. Jonathan could see a puzzled look forming on the gnomes face, as if he was really unsure of what to say.

'Freddy, that's my name,' he mumbled hurriedly.

'Where are you from? Do you live near here?' Jonathan asked, becoming more and more curious.

'I live on the top of Ecton Hill in the Manifold Valley,' Freddy replied quietly.

Now Jonathan knew a bit about Ecton Hill, again thanks to Joe who was always ready to pass on interesting bits of information, whether it was about the history of Casterne Hall or the local countryside. He had told Jonathan that in the eighteenth century Ecton Hill had been a bustling copper mine, employing over ten thousand miners. It was mined for over 300 years and was now one of the largest disused copper mines in Britain.

'But there are no homes on the top,' said Jonathan.

'There is one,' answered Freddy. 'My home is in the trig point. I'm a Trignome.'

Jonathan looked completely baffled. He seemed to forget about all his troubles and became totally focussed on this fascinating little creature in front of him. He'd only seen a picture of a trig point in a book at school. He thought back to it now and remembered the little door at the front.

'Of course,' he exclaimed. 'It makes perfect sense, why

has no one thought about this before?' Jonathan looked more closely at Freddy. His long brown coat was torn at the back where he had tried so hard to wriggle free from the rock. The large buttons were undone and Jonathan could see Freddy was wearing a red pullover underneath with what looked like black corduroy trousers. His pot belly hung over them like a balloon. His funny pointed shoes seemed out of sorts with the rest of him. His spikey hair was white and stuck out at odd angles from beneath his brown pointed hat.

Jonathan noticed Freddy was shifting about from one foot to the other, looking increasingly uncomfortable. He thought about what Freddy had just told him and began to wonder how many other people knew about Trignomes.

'What about you?' he asked Jonathan hastily. 'What's a young boy doing out here all alone?'

Chapter Two

Two Weeks Earlier

Jonathan sat gazing out of the window, wavy blond hair hung around his face, blowing backwards with the breeze to reveal his youth and his soft blue eyes. In the distance he could see the steep mass of Thorpe Cloud dominating the horizon with the beautiful countryside spread before it. The lush fields were scattered with sheep, the little lambs almost skipping along to get back to their mothers. Others seemed to be playing together without a care in the world. They were grazing amongst the huge, old, majestic trees, with their leaves reflecting varying shades of green in the sunshine. The grassy mountain, interspersed with the grey limestone rocks, rose up high above them. Jonathan often stared up at it and wondered if one day he would see a spaceship landing on the flat top. He imagined the aliens coming down into the village and taking him away on an exciting adventure. But that wasn't going to happen any time soon. In a few days' time it would be Good Friday and the traditional carrying of the big cross would begin. It would be taken all the way up Thorpe Cloud and placed on the summit.

Jonathan had watched it being carried out of the village many times, but last year he had wondered why it attracted so many visitors. Did it hold some special power that he knew nothing about? It was something that had been playing on his mind over the last months, so a few weeks ago he had asked Mrs Milson if they could walk up with the cross. He didn't tell her why he wanted to, but he just felt he had to see for himself if there was anything really special about it. Perhaps it would somehow help him find what was missing from his life. He had read a story once about a magic stone that granted a wish to the person who held it. Maybe the cross had magical powers too. The more he thought about this, the more certain he became that it was true. With this in mind, Jonathan decided that following the procession of the cross to the summit of Thorpe Cloud may be worth a try. After all, it couldn't make him feel worse than he already did.

Unfortunately, Mrs Milson had said she had to work, so that was the end of that. She had looked at him and laughed, her soft skin wrinkling up around her eyes.

'Why on earth do you want to follow the cross all that way? It's quite a trek for a young lad you know.'

'I just thought it might be fun,' replied Jonathan, shrugging his shoulders to show he didn't really care too much one way or the other.

Mrs Milson tugged at his arm and cuddled him close. Her red hair (which changed colour quite frequently) shone in the sunlight as it curled and fell softly, adding to the gentleness radiating from her warm hazel eyes. He looked up at her and smiled. He knew he was lucky to have such a loving foster mum, but somehow it just wasn't enough.

It was a few nights later that Jonathan thought of a plan to get up to the cross without anyone knowing he had gone. He had convinced himself that it did indeed have magical powers and it was going to be able to help him. He just had a couple of weeks to get everything ready.

For as long as he could remember Jonathan had wanted to change his life. Now he had reached his ninth birthday and still things were just the same. Why couldn't he share the same experiences his friends talked about at school? All the things they did with their mums and dads, the tiresome squabbling with a sister or brother. How he longed to be like them. He kept trying to figure out why he had to be different from all the other children he knew. Why couldn't he be with his real mum and dad?

Of course he had friends who lived with their mum and only saw their dad at weekends, or for a night or two in the week. Others had never seen their dad, but they didn't seem to feel like Jonathan. They were content to live with their mum and brothers and sisters and not worry about where their father was. Then there was Annie and Lizzie. They regularly came to stay with their aunt and uncle who lived in a cottage a few doors away. Their dad was a Royal Marine and he often seemed to be away on active service in Iraq, Afghanistan and who knows where else. They had told Jonathan how horrible they felt when their dad was away and how worried they were that he might be hurt or killed and they may never see him again. Jonathan could understand how they felt, even though his situation was so different. He knew what it was like knowing you may never see one of your parents again. It was precisely this feeling that he couldn't really get his head around. He wanted to change things so he could see his mum. Maybe her circumstances were better now and maybe she even had other children. He could have a brother or sister and he could be living with his real family. His mum had no way of knowing where he was, so that was why she hadn't found him. All these thoughts went round and round in Jonathan's head. If everyone else lived in a proper family then he should be able to as well. He knew he couldn't just let this one go. He had to find an answer that would help him have the life he thought he was entitled to. It was for exactly this reason he had decided to take a chance and make his way to the cross. Believing it had magical powers, just like the stone in the story, made him feel sure it would be able to help him be reunited with his family. If it brought him a way forward then that was a start.

Chapter Three

As people were gathering in the village, getting ready for the procession of the cross, Mrs Milson was leaving for work. She was in charge of the catering team at Casterne Hall, a large manor house, which apart from being featured in several films, was also a venue that could be hired for weddings and special events. As Mrs Milson drove the five minute journey to Casterne Hall, Jonathan sat in the front seat deep in thought. They entered the long, steep, winding driveway, glimpsing two of the chimneys half way up. Around the last bend Jonathan never ceased to be struck by the vastness of the grey stone house and the many Georgian windows adorning the three-storey building. The two wide centre chimneys dominated the skyline above the dark grey tiled roof. He had often wondered what it must be like to live in such an enormous house, with so many bedrooms on the two upper floors. The rooms on the ground floor were very grand. He was sure the whole of the downstairs of Mrs Milson's cottage would fit into one of these magnificent rooms with their large fireplaces and high ceilings. Mrs Milson didn't drive through the big iron gates at the front of the house, but instead went around the back and parked in the courtyard by the stable block.

'How you doing?' yelled Joe from across the yard.

'Fine thanks,' Jonathan replied, keeping his head down as he made his way towards the back door. It wasn't that he didn't like talking to Joe. Joe was a kind man and had a smile for everyone. It was hard to tell how old he was as his face had that weather-beaten look that you get from spending a lot of time outdoors, making him look older than he probably was. His thin grey hair was cut just below his ears and receded slightly, revealing his wrinkled forehead. He was head gardener at Casterne Hall and had always had time for Jonathan, letting him run around the grounds when it wasn't being hired out and telling him a thing or two about the history of the place. Today, Jonathan didn't want to stop and talk, not to Joe or anyone. He was on a mission. He had to get the last of his food supplies. He felt a bit uncomfortable about what he had been doing over the last few days and he didn't need any distractions. He was now more determined than ever to get away and reach the top of Thorpe Cloud and nothing was going to stop him.

He'd already managed to take a local map that one of the guests had left. That was a real find; it was almost like a sign telling him now was his time to embark on an adventure. Stocking up on food supplies was easier than he had thought. With all the gatherings that went on, particularly the weddings, food was never far away and there were always plenty of leftovers! Jonathan had been able to slide numerous pieces of roast beef and chicken into a napkin and then carefully place it under his jumper. Roast potatoes were another easy target, along with pieces of fruit and bread rolls; he had just about all he needed. With a swiftness of hand that any magician would have been proud of, he'd packed them into his school bag. Once home in the evenings he would carefully hide them in his rucksack, stored discreetly under his bed.

The time was drawing near. He spent many a night too excited to sleep, going over the route again and again. He'd found a torch in one of the sheds at Casterne Hall. He didn't see it as stealing, just borrowing. It was the final thing he needed; now he was all set. School had broken up for the holidays, so no one would miss him there. Mrs Milson, on the other hand, was more of a problem. Then the solution came to him.

'Mrs Milson.'

'Yes love.'

'Jack's asked me to stay over at his for a couple of days. I've got a note from his mum.' Jonathan had scribbled a few words down whilst at school. He knew he would need more than his 'say so' to convince her that it would be ok.

Mrs Milson studied the note carefully. 'Well, I suppose that will be ok.' She wasn't normally such a pushover, but Jonathan had timed the request just perfectly. One of the staff had not come in to work, so Mrs Milson had a lot of extra things to do. She was in such a fluster that she was not giving the situation her full attention. Had she, things may have turned out very differently.

Chapter Four

Monday afternoon had arrived and Jonathan was ready to go. He had packed his rucksack very carefully, with his food supplies towards the bottom just in case Mrs Milson wanted to take quick look. Luckily, she had to be at Casterne Hall by 3pm to prepare for an evening wedding reception. She was quite concerned about not being at home when Jack's mother arrived. Jonathan had said he was being collected at 9pm. Mrs Milson thought this was rather late, so Jonathan came up with the excuse that the family were on their way back from visiting relatives. Of course, unbeknown to her, the real reason Jonathan did not want to set off too early was because he needed the cover of darkness to avoid being noticed. A young boy walking on their own might well arouse suspicion to anyone passing by.

'Well, I'll be off then love,' said Mrs Milson rather reluctantly. 'You have a good time and remember your manners.'

'Don't worry I will,' smiled Jonathan. 'Bye.'

Mrs Milson gave him a long hug and ruffled his thick blond hair with her hand. 'I'll miss you,' she said softly. 'Bye love.' She rushed out of the door and Jonathan closed it quickly behind her.

The next few hours seemed to go by so slowly. Jonathan sat very quietly in the sitting room, watching the hands of the brass carriage clock on the mantelpiece gradually going round.

He was feeling more apprehensive than excited as the time approached for him to leave. Doubt crept into his mind. What if he got lost or fell and hurt himself? He didn't really know what the terrain would be like as he had never been up Thorpe Cloud before.

He thought about Mrs Milson. He had been back with her for four years now and he knew she loved him. It wasn't quite the same now Mr Milson was gone, but he knew that she treated him like he was her own son.

Like many of the cottages in the village of Ilam, Mrs Milson's was very picturesque, with its pitched tiled roof and small leaded windows, mimicking the style of a Swiss alpine cottage rather than what you may normally expect to see in a more traditional English village. Honeysuckle grew up around the archway to the front door, adding a welcoming feel when it was in blossom, with the sweet scent emitting from the pretty flowers. Jonathan remembered feeling so safe when he returned here from his previous foster home.

He had never really known his mum and dad. All he knew was that he had been left by the entrance to the hospital in Ashbourne when he was two years old. He had been fast asleep and wrapped up very tightly in a rough old blanket. He had obviously been cared for as he was clean and warm, but he was a little undernourished and his clothes were threadbare in places. There had been a little note pinned to the blanket. The writing was scratchy but it was legible. It said:

This is Jonathan. He is two years old. Please take care of him and find him a good home. I can't look after him any more.

His mother disappeared and the police had never been able to trace her.

Mr and Mrs Milson had not been able to have children of

their own and so had decided to become foster parents around the same time as Jonathan had been abandoned. They took care of him for six months and then he was given to a younger couple with a view to them adopting him. Mr and Mrs Milson had been heartbroken at the time. They had tried so hard to adopt Jonathan themselves but had been told they were too old.

For two and a half years Jonathan lived with his new family. Mr and Mrs Milson couldn't bring themselves to foster another child; the pain of losing Jonathan had been too great. However, Jonathan's new mum and dad had decided to postpone the adoption until they were absolutely sure it was what they wanted. Jonathan was completely unaware of the dilemmas they were having. As far as he was concerned, he was home and they were his mum and dad. Just before he was about to start school they dropped the bombshell. The lady he called mum was going to have a baby; something she had thought would never happen. Now they could have their own child they no longer wanted to adopt Jonathan, so social services were called and another foster home had to be found for him.

As a temporary measure social services contacted Mr and Mrs Milson in the hope that they would take Jonathan until a more permanent home could be found. Of course they took him back with open arms, and due to the shortage of foster parents, Jonathan had remained there ever since. About a year later Mr Milson died after a long struggle with cancer. Mrs Milson was devastated, but having Jonathan with her helped her to overcome her loss. She was terrified that Jonathan would be taken away, but it was decided that as he was so settled and happy and doing well at the village school, it was kinder to leave him in Ilam, at least for the time being.

So Jonathan began his visits to Casterne Hall. Without Mr Milson, it was impossible to leave him at home on his own, so Mrs Milson took him with her to work whenever he was not in school. He loved the huge house and gardens. Joe was always pleased to see him, as were the other people who worked at the hall. He tried hard to stay out of the way when Mrs Milson was busy preparing the food for the guests. She always took plenty of things for him to do, and in the summer he could spend more time outside with Joe, or exploring on his own; as long as the visitors weren't in the grounds. The arrangement worked well and as Mrs Milson was worth her weight in gold, no one at the hall minded.

Chapter Five

The grandfather clock in the corner struck nine. Jonathan jumped! Despite watching the time so carefully his edginess had got the better of him. He got up slowly and reached for his rucksack. After putting on his school coat (the warmest and only one he had), he walked purposefully to the front door and turned the latch.

Jonathan took a deep breath and set off down the road, trying to look confident so anyone who saw him would think he was just on his way home. He rushed along as quickly as he could; only stopping once when he saw someone approaching. He stood in the doorway of a little cottage, pretending to be waiting to be let in. That seemed to do the trick. The stranger paid no attention to Jonathan and he was able to carry on with his journey unchallenged. He took on a brisk pace, wanting to get out of the village as quickly as he could. He made his way along the lane, following the River Dove downstream. He was very wary of any traffic that might pass by. This was not so much out of concern for his safety, but anyone seeing him alone now would surely be suspicious as he was heading away from the village. Fortunately, the lane was quiet and he was soon stepping through the gate and onto the path that took him across the open fields. At first it was steep and uneven, but then it levelled out onto a footpath that took him past the Izakk Walton's Hotel. The lights from the windows shed a feeling of warmth on the ever-dimming surroundings, not quite reaching the shadowy outline of Bunster Hill on the far side of the path.

Soon Jonathan descended into the car park at Dovedale. He breathed a sigh of relief – so far so good. He could barely make out the signpost to the stepping stones, but there was still just enough light to show him the way. He followed the path, not venturing over the wooden footbridge, but preferring to be more adventurous and use the stepping stones further ahead. There had been quite a lot of rain in recent weeks so the River Dove was running fairly high. However, the stepping stones had not been closed off as he knew they had been at times during the winter, so Jonathan assumed he would be able to cross safely.

He jumped from stone to stone, enjoying the sound of the water splashing against the sides of the large grey boulders. He imagined the noise to be similar to the sea lapping against a rocky shore. Thorpe Cloud towered above him. He could almost feel the huge limestone hill beckoning to him. A shudder went through him. Was it the cold or was he a little bit afraid?

Chapter Six

Freddy had listened in silence as Jonathan had relayed his life story and how he had come to be in Dovedale.

'You are remarkably determined for a young boy,' said Freddy quietly.

As he put his hand out towards Jonathan darkness seemed to envelop him, and a black wispy cloud circled all around him. As fast as it had appeared it was gone again. Jonathan didn't see any of this as his head was in his hands. Freddy's voice altered and took on a much rougher tone. Had Jonathan not had such tear-filled eyes, he may well have noticed that Freddy's eyes had changed too. They were no longer black but an emerald green, and they were bulging out of his head more than ever.

'Determined, determined. Yes, that's exactly what we need,' Freddy expressed loudly. 'We must get moving, there is no time to lose.'

'Why, where are we going?' asked Jonathan, sniffing and wiping his tears away with the back of his hand.

'You'll see. I will explain on the way.'

Before Jonathan could collect his thoughts Freddy had set off. He moved incredibly quickly for one so small, almost hopping from one foot to the other. Jonathan had to run to catch up with him. They were at the bottom of the steps on the other side of Lover's Leap in no time and the path now wound alongside the river again.

Soon the pillars of Tissington Spires rose ahead of them; a magnificent backdrop of limestone with the contrast of the green trees and bushes interspersed between them. Jonathan was craning his neck so he could peer upwards towards the sky, the height of the pillars seemingly endless. Suddenly he caught site of some climbers just starting an ascent up one of the spires. Panic consumed him and he stood motionless.

Freddy had spotted the climbers too and realised they needed to make themselves scarce for a while. This trip wasn't going according to plan, although at least he had the boy now and that would make it a whole lot easier. Nevertheless, it did have its downside as he was quite conspicuous and could easily attract attention. This was something Freddy couldn't afford to let happen. Quickly he motioned to Jonathan to follow him, putting his finger to his lips to indicate the need to be quiet. Freddy led them carefully towards the spires, trying to get Jonathan to dodge behind as many bushes as he could to avoid being seen. Unbeknown to Freddy the climbers were a relatively inexperienced group, apart from their leader, and they were listening to instructions so intensely you could have tapped them on the shoulder and they wouldn't have noticed!

Not long after they had passed the climbers, Freddy heard more voices in the distance. The hearing capacity of a Trignome is far more astute than that of a human, so Jonathan was completely unaware of the people approaching. There was only one thing to do; walking along here in the daylight was bound to lead to disaster. They couldn't possibly avoid being seen with so many walkers visiting the Dale. Freddy signalled to Jonathan, pointing to a narrow path on the right.

'You haven't told me where we are going yet,' moaned Jonathan, who was beginning to feel a little hungry. 'I've got some food in my bag. Why don't we stop and have a bite to eat?'

'Do be quiet, you idiotic child,' Freddy whispered angrily, his emerald eyes glaring at Jonathan. 'There are people coming and we have to hide in the cave.'

'What cave?' he asked Freddy.

'Reynard's Cave,' retorted Freddy. 'Not that it makes any difference to you. Just get on with it or we will never get there.'

Jonathan was so taken aback by the aggressive tone Freddy had used he decided not to argue, but followed him meekly up the path. He had walked along the river many times, both with his class at school and Mr and Mrs Milson. He knew there were caves around the area, but had always thought it was too difficult to walk to any of them.

Something else was bothering Jonathan too. He was sure that Freddy's eyes were black, but just a minute ago there were two huge green eyes bulging out of his head. Had he imagined that? As he was pondering over this the path became very steep and stony. His pace slowed considerably, much to the irritation of Freddy.

'Would you get a move on,' he yelled at Jonathan. 'We have to get to the safety of the cave.'

'I'm going as quickly as I can,' Jonathan panted.

A huge arched entrance stood before him with bundles of bushy plants clinging onto the limestone. The area was surrounded by trees, young and old, with their clusters of small green leaves unfolding as they burst from their buds. The path was really quite tricky to negotiate; as it got steeper it became more difficult to choose a solid footing in places. Jonathan knew that if he fell he could seriously injure himself. He tried hard to concentrate on where he was putting his feet and not to think about falling.

Jonathan realised now was not the time to question Freddy anymore. He tried to convince himself that Freddy was really a kind Trignome and was only getting angry because he was worried about their safety. After all, Jonathan was not ready to go back to Ilam yet. However, a nagging doubt was beginning to creep into his mind, but this was soon put aside when he saw the magnificent sight ahead.

Through the archway, Jonathan could see the small cave. He scrambled up the large stones and was quickly at the entrance. Once inside, the cave got narrower and the roof lowered, making it feel dark and enclosed. The wet walls were green with algae, and as Jonathan held out his reddened hands, he felt they were as cold as marble. They almost looked like gnarled trees knitted together. The floor was very uneven and Jonathan couldn't see anywhere that would be comfortable to sit down and wait.

'We need to stay here until the end of the day,' stated Freddy. 'We can't risk being seen and if any walkers should come up here, we can hide in the trees. I will hear them coming a long time before they get here.'

'You still haven't told me what we are doing,' said Jonathan, misguidedly thinking Freddy was no longer angry.

A blind rage swept over Freddy like a fire and he roared back at Jonathan.

'You are here to do as I say. We have to get to the Lion's Head. There is something inside the rock that I need and you can help me get it. Now no more questions; I've said too much already.'

Jonathan stared at Freddy in disbelief. Could this be the same little Trignome he rescued from the rock and poured his heart out to? A sudden sense of fear ran through him like the chill of an icy wind.

'If I'm not back in Ilam tomorrow people will start looking for me,' Jonathan ventured cautiously. 'I have to be back in the morning or else Mrs Milson will know I didn't stay at my friend's.'

'That's hardly my problem is it? If you do as you are told this will all be over with by tonight, and you can go back to your precious Ilam, although from what you have told me I can't see why you would want to.'

Freddy moved to the entrance of the cave, leaving Jonathan alone with his thoughts.

His eyes followed Freddy and he gazed out of the dark, cold cave. It was like looking through a window. A beautiful abounding landscape stretched before him through the archway below. A mass of trees with their leaves glistening in the sunlight was indeed a beautiful sight. Usually, this would have made him feel happy, but not today.

Jonathan was suddenly too concerned to feel anything but fear. What would he have to do for this gnome? Would it be dangerous? Did he want to go back to Ilam? Where else would he go? All these questions flooded his mind. As he sat wondering what to do, his thoughts drifted to Mrs Milson.

Her ruby red cheeks, her beaming smile, the softness of her skin, the feeling of security it gave him when she cuddled him close. These images filled him with such a sense of sadness and longing and with it brought the realisation that he could never contemplate not going back to her. She had given so much of her life to him and treated him like he was her own child. How silly and ungrateful he had been. With a sense of urgency he knew he must get back to Ilam. He would tell Mrs Milson the truth and she would understand. Perhaps if he talked to her about how he was really feeling, she could help him feel better.

Jonathan had made his decision; it was time to leave the cave and make his way back home. As he stood up Freddy spun round and glared at him.

'Where do you think you're going? Sit back down and keep quiet, we've got a long wait.'

'I'm going home,' said Jonathan rather nervously. Something about the way Freddy looked at him made him feel very uneasy.

'You are doing no such thing,' yelled Freddy. 'I've already told you what we need to do, so sit back down and eat some of that food you said you had.'

Jonathan took a deep breath. After all, Freddy couldn't stop him leaving.

'No, I've made my mind up. I don't want to help you; I just want to go home.'

As Jonathan approached the entrance to the cave, something strange began to happen. The archway filled with a black wispy cloud that had descended from nowhere. As it got nearer Freddy seemed to be shrinking backwards, looking more and more like the Trignome he'd first met, with black eyes staring at the cloud in fear. As Jonathan reached the large stones, the cloud suddenly enveloped him and he couldn't move. He felt himself swirling round and round, even though his feet were stuck firmly to the ground. His head was spinning and an evil cackle filled his ears. The sound was deafening and he brought his hands up to try and block it out. He was filled with a fear as dark and deep as night as he felt himself falling and drifting away.

Chapter Seven

A steady south-westerly wind was blowing gently across the sky and the moon was full. This meant the conditions were perfect for Geoffrey to visit his dear friend Jasper on Selworthy Beacon in Exmoor.

Geoffrey was a Trignome who lived in the trig point on the top of Whernside, in the Yorkshire Dales. Whernside is the highest mountain in Yorkshire and easy to identify as it is characterised by the long ridge that runs along its top. Geoffrey had lived in the trig point all his life. At first with his parents and now, since they had both died, he lived alone. The concrete pillar was originally built to help form a detailed mapping system of Great Britain. Not long after the first one was built in 1936, Trignomes had made them their homes right across the country. On Whernside, the trig point was positioned behind a dry stone wall, which often provided walkers with shelter from the cold wind. Although the area just outside the trig point was quite stony, grass and heather were not far away. It was in these areas where Geoffrey was able to rummage around and find food. He lived on a diet of mainly berries, stewed heather and gorse, and very healthy he looked on it too! His light brown hair lay like a thick mop on his head, with wispy curls hanging down over his large hazel eyes. His bushy eyebrows seemed almost too big for his gentle face and his soft reddish beard clung closely to his skin. At a height of 13cm, he was just about able to enter the door of the trig point without having to stoop to avoid banging his head. Once inside his home there was enough space for four or five Trignomes, and Geoffrey hoped that one day he would have a family of his own.

He'd been busy making some berry jam when he received the message from Jasper. He heard the familiar sound and rushed to see who was calling him. You see, Trignomes have a very unique way of communicating with each other over long distances. They use a combination of sound and light signals that humans cannot hear or see, but if it is dark, then the ball of light can be seen by anyone. Have you ever looked up at the night sky and thought you were seeing a shooting star? You may be right. However, it could also be one Trignome sending a message to another. The minute a Trignome hears the message signal, he has to catch the light ball to receive the message in full. It hovers over the trig point until the Trignome can safely retrieve it.

Geoffrey checked to see if anyone was nearby. It was all clear. Once outside he saw the light ball heading his way.

'Tae mai,' he called, whilst reaching up and cupping his hands to receive the ball. When safely back inside his home, Geoffrey spoke once more.

'Tuwhera.'

The light ball quickly expanded, lifting itself out of Geoffrey's hands as it hung in mid-air beside him.

'Geoffrey, me old chum. It's high time you paid us a visit.' Jasper's ruddy face beamed out at Geoffrey. His deep black eyes and his curling black moustache making his face appear as friendly as ever.

'Joan worries about you spending too much time on your own and Harry and Hazel have really missed you!' boomed

44

Jasper. 'Weather looks good, so why not come over for a few days; we'd love to see you.'

Geoffrey smiled. He was very fond of his dear friend, and along with Joan and the children they were just like family to him. He was delighted to receive the invitation and Jasper was right, the south-westerly wind would certainly aid his flight down to Exmoor. He sent a message back to Jasper straight away and quickly finished making his berry jam so he could get on with the more important task of packing for his journey.

As he was about to start sorting through his clothes, he checked again to see if anyone was on top of the mountain. The 'look out', as it was called, was a very clever mechanism invented in 1937 by Gilbert Trignome who lived on Snowdon in North Wales. He had soon realised that there was great danger in Trignomes leaving their homes without knowing if any humans were near the trig point. He tried various ways of solving this problem and eventually came up with the 'look out'. It consisted of a tube-like structure that came down from the centre of the metal plate on the top of the outside of the trig point, through to the ceiling inside the living area. When the small wooden handle was turned, a little periscope would pop up through to the outside. Like the light ball, this was invisible to the human eye in daylight and enabled Trignomes to have a 360 degree view of the surrounding area. Luckily, it was very seldom for walkers to be there when it was dark, so Trignomes had been able to leave their homes undetected for all these years.

When Geoffrey looked out he saw three people heading away back down the mountain. He hoped that once he had finished his packing, it would be safe to leave straight away.

Little did he know that soon his life would be changed forever…

Chapter Eight

Annie and Lizzie were also packing up their things ready to go up to the Yorkshire Dales for a few days with their mum and dad. Their dad had two weeks leave from his tour of duty in Afghanistan. After a week at home, he had decided it would be good to take the family to Yorkshire to have a complete break before returning to his camp in Sangin.

'What shall we take to Aunty Sheila's and Uncle Alan's?' asked Lizzie.

Annie smiled at her twin sister. Lizzie's clear blue eyes shone with excitement as she looked up and brushed her long blonde curls over her shoulder with the back of her hand.

'I think we should definitely take some extra jumpers and jeans. It always seems so much colder up there,' replied Annie.

At the age of eight, the twins still liked to dress the same a lot of the time. Although not identical, people who didn't know them still found it hard to tell them apart. The girls thought it was fun when they were able to keep people guessing as to who was who. Their aunt and uncle lived in Ilam in the Peak District; only two and a half hours drive south of the Yorkshire Dales. Mum and Dad had decided it would be a good idea to call in there for a few days on the way back. Dad would drop them off and then drive straight back to the army camp. Aunty Sheila was their mum's sister and they often visited her and Uncle Alan. Sometimes their dad came and other times, when he was off on a tour of duty, they would go without him. It seemed to give their mum more security to be with her sister for a while when their dad was away. She always said it helped to take her mind off worrying about him.

Annie and Lizzie didn't like their dad being away either. They spent many restless nights each thinking something terrible was going to happen, each wondering what if he never came back, or if he got really hurt? They would lay awake and hold each other's hand across the small divide between their twin beds. On a bad night they would drift in and out of sleep and sometimes their mum would find them cuddled up together in the same bed in the morning. It was more comforting to hold on to each other. They both knew what the other was thinking and feeling. They knew how to give each other strength and how to pretend to be strong for their mum who always seemed to lose so much weight when their dad was away, only picking at her food yet demanding that Annie and Lizzie ate up every scrap.

This time their dad had recorded some bedtime stories for them to listen to. It felt so good to hear his voice each night, and if they closed their eyes they could imagine he was sitting on the edge of the bed, pulling funny faces as he read with different accents.

They lived in the Royal Navy Camp in Taunton, Somerset. There were lots of families there, all in the same situation when 40 Commando were on a tour of duty. The twins were only allowed to watch certain television programmes when their dad was away. Their mum was very selective and Annie and Lizzie never questioned her. They knew she didn't want them to be worried about the news reports they might hear about Afghanistan. It was just one of those situations when children seem to be able to accept certain decisions and adults remain oblivious to the fact that the children know the real reason behind them.

Although the girls were dreading their dad going away again, they were looking forward to another visit to Ilam. They had become really good friends with a boy there called Jonathan. Whenever they met up they spent hours sharing their news. Jonathan was always so keen to hear about what Annie and Lizzie had been up to and where their dad had been. He had a special way about him that always seemed to show the girls a depth of understanding about their situation that none of their friends at home seemed to share. He'd listen to their worries and concerns about their dad and the girls would return home feeling so much happier.

They in turn would listen to Jonathan, who seemed so sad inside, even though his foster mum was such a nice lady. Although he would say to them that they were the only people he could talk to, they never really felt that they had helped him to feel happier. As hard as they tried, they always left wishing there was something more they could do. Still, they managed to have a lot of fun together when they weren't in deep conversation. They would spend hours playing in Ilam Park or sitting by the river watching the ducks bobbing up and down on the water.

'Did you know that Dad wants to walk up three different mountains when we are in Yorkshire?' Annie asked her sister as she zipped up the case.

'Yes!' laughed Lizzie. 'He knows we won't complain because we want him to have a good time before he goes back. I'm sure it will be fun though, and there are always the ice creams to look forward to!'

'That's true.' Annie smiled to herself as she thought about

that. Her parents had always been particularly generous with the offer of ice creams when a long walk was involved. The girls now took this for granted, whatever part of the country they happened to be walking in and whatever the weather!

'Let's tell Mum and Dad we are ready shall we? Dad will be very impressed we managed to pack so quickly,' Lizzie said happily as she raced downstairs with her twin sister scurrying behind her.

Chapter Nine

'Oh, where did I put my whistle?' Geoffrey asked himself as he frantically searched his rather untidy abode. The cushions were upturned on his old peach sofa, pots and pans remained on the wooden draining board and as for his bed, well, that was a sight to behold with the covers thrown back and clothes draped over every corner.

Geoffrey was getting ready to visit Jasper and as he started to pack his backpack, he realised he didn't have his whistle. When a Trignome travels a whistle is essential, as if they find themselves in trouble using it will alert any Trignome nearby and give them the location of the gnome in need of help. It would be foolish to travel without it, although the need to use it was very rare.

In one last desperate effort to find it Geoffrey bent down to look under his unmade bed. The shiny silver birch whistle was there for all to see.

'Ah, thank goodness for that,' exclaimed Geoffrey. 'At last I can be on my way.'

Geoffrey was now running late. He should have left a few hours ago. Around dawn was always the safest time for Trignomes to travel; it lessened the risk of being seen by a human. For Geoffrey, the last few hours of desperately trying to find his whistle had made him lose all track of time and his instinctively cautious nature appeared to have vanished. His total focus seemed to be on getting to Jasper's as soon as he could. He was not one to break his promise and he had said he would be arriving today, so today it would be. He put on his thick jacket and pulled his black woolly hat over his ears. Without a moment's thought he threw caution to the wind and marched out of his door, backpack packed to the brim on his back.

As he closed the door behind him Geoffrey came nose to nose with the most beautiful human he had ever seen. Bright blue eyes as clear as crystal were staring into his with amazement and disbelief. He froze. Never in his life had he come anywhere near this close to a human before. Of course, he'd often seen them at a distance and heard their conversations as they chatted around the trig point, but he knew the rules; no Trignome must ever reveal themselves to humans.

The sudden appearance of a wet black nose made Geoffrey squeal like a pig. As quick as a flash he tried to run, but he found himself held down under the soft pad of the dog's paw. He couldn't move.

'Elsa, no!' The little girl reached over and gently cupped Geoffrey into her hands and pulled him close to her chest. As he looked up he thought he must have knocked his head. Instead of one beautiful face he saw two, with two pairs of sparkling blue eyes gazing at him. He shook his head to try and clear it, but there they were; two faces as if they were one.

'Don't worry,' said Lizzie kindly, 'we aren't going to hurt you.' She smiled at this strange little creature with his woolly hat pulled right down over his head. She could just make out his large hazel eyes.

Geoffrey had no idea what to do next. He knew he couldn't escape; the dog would be far too quick for him and it was too late to pretend not to be a living gnome. After all, they had already seen him move and heard him squeal!

'My name's Lizzie,' the little girl continued, 'and this is my twin sister Annie. We were just hiding from our mum and dad when you popped out of the trig point. Do you live in there?'

Lizzie could see a look of panic spread across Geoffrey's face. This soon turned to bewilderment as he drew his eyebrows together, as if trying to work out a difficult puzzle.

'Well, mmm, well actually, mmm, well – yes, I do,' Geoffrey bumbled quietly. 'Are your parents with you?'

'Yes they are, but we have run on ahead,' replied Annie. She realised that this news had made the little creature even more agitated. 'You don't need to worry; they won't be here for at least 5 minutes,' she said reassuringly.

'Oh, well in that case would you like to come inside and see my little home?' Geoffrey sounded almost relieved to hear that the girls' parents were not about to suddenly appear and he seemed keen to show them inside the trig point.

'Really, we'd love to,' the girls replied excitedly.

'Ok, we all need to hold hands and you will have to have to hold on to the dog as well.'

'Oh, that's ok,' said Annie. 'Elsa will be fine out here for a few minutes.'

'Well it's not quite that simple,' hesitated Geoffrey. 'You see, if Elsa starts barking your parents might hear her and think something is wrong. If they rush up here and see you with me then I will be in real trouble. You are the first humans ever to see me and I'm not sure your parents will be able to keep my existence a secret. I'm rather hoping that you will be able to though, otherwise other people may come and harm me or take my home away.'

'Oh gosh, of course we won't tell anyone,' the twins responded quickly, feeling very important and proud that this little creature put so much trust in them, even though they had only just met.

The girls did as they were told as quickly as they could, gazing expectantly at Geoffrey.

'Close your eyes,' Geoffrey whispered.

As they did so Geoffrey began to chant, 'nohinohi, nohinohi, nohinohi.'

Without thinking Geoffrey had closed his eyes too. He had never used this enchantment before and had no idea if it would work. His grandfather had taught it to him many years ago. He'd told Geoffrey that he had used it only once in his lifetime. He had been spotted by a fox when out collecting grasses and would most certainly have been eaten had he not uttered the enchantment. The fox became very small and was so bewildered it gave Geoffrey's grandfather time to escape. Of course, never in a million years would his grandfather expect him to use it on humans!

'Ooooh,' squealed the girls.

Geoffrey opened his eyes. It had worked; they were all smaller than him. 'Quick, follow me and keep hold of your dog, she must come with us.'

They all hurried towards the little door in the trig point. Geoffrey waved his hand in a circular motion and as it opened he gently pushed the girls and dog inside.

'Wow, this is amazing!' Lizzie exclaimed. 'Who'd have ever thought that all this was underneath the trig point? Do you live alone?'

'Yes,' replied Geoffrey anxiously.

Annie thought he still looked rather nervous and worried. His eyebrows were once more drawn together and his mouth was twitching from side to side. However, she was so thrilled to be inside the trig point she quickly put her concerns to the back of her mind, although she was aware he was watching them as they ran around his cosy home, excitedly exchanging little notions with each other.

Geoffrey smiled; it was lovely to hear their little squeaky voices resonating through the house. Annie glanced across at him and saw his smile that was somehow tinged with sadness. It was almost as if he was missing something or someone.

The howl from the dog brought Geoffrey and Annie back to reality.

'Elsa, Elsa,' cried Annie. 'You're shivering.' Concern flooded over the faces of the twins as they looked across to Geoffrey, pleading with him to help them.

'It's alright,' reassured Geoffrey. 'It's just that she has got a bit disorientated and she feels a bit frightened. She'll soon settle down. Geoffrey smiled at the two little girls and they smiled back. Their blue eyes sparkled with a mixture of wonder and uncertainty. Their long blonde hair hung below their shoulders, partly tied back with a small black band. They were dressed identically in a short hooded dark blue denim jacket with slightly lighter blue jeans. Both were wearing black and green canvas walking boots with thick socks protruding out over the top. One had a blue pair, the other pink. There were only small differences in their facial features, so the socks were the only thing that really helped to tell them apart.

As Elsa started to sniff around the house, the girls became

more curious again. 'What's your name and what sort of creature are you?' asked Lizzie tentatively.

'Oh, how rude of me not to introduce myself. I'm Geoffrey and I'm a Trignome.'

Soon the girls had learned all about Trignomes. Geoffrey seemed much more relaxed now and words were streaming out from his mouth without him giving anything a second thought.

'There are many of us all over the country,' he explained. 'Some of us live alone and some live with families. In fact, I was just off to visit one of my friends when I bumped into you.'

'Really, how exciting. Where were you going, if you don't mind us asking?' Annie spoke very quietly, her face fixed on Geoffrey's. Both girls were hanging onto his every word.

'Well, it was going to be quite a long journey. I was off to Exmoor. Have you heard of it?'

'Yes, we have,' the girls replied together. Lizzie then enlightened Geoffrey a bit more. 'We only live about forty-five minutes away from the edge of Exmoor. Our parents love walking and we have stayed in a campsite in a place called Horner. Is that where your friend lives?'

'No,' said Geoffrey rather too quickly, 'but it's not far from there.' He was certainly not going to divulge Jasper's home to these two; he had to be sure he could trust them. He'd already jeopardised every Trignome around the country and he had to think of a way to undo the harm that could arise from his mistake.

'Lizzie, don't you think Mum and Dad will be wondering where we are by now? They weren't that far behind us and we've been here ages.' Annie looked at her sister; a flash of alarm had crossed her face. Clearly her concern for her parents was greater than her curiosity.

'Oh, yes, I suppose you are right,' said Lizzie rather reluctantly. 'We should get back.'

Geoffrey knew that he couldn't let them go yet. He hadn't worked out how he was going to get them to keep his secret. The only way to keep them longer was to tell them more. He hesitated, but there was no other option.

'Don't worry; they will have no idea you have been here. It's the time you see, it's different.'

'What do you mean, different?' asked Lizzie.

'Well, it sounds complicated and I don't really understand it myself. It's just what my grandfather told me,' explained Geoffrey.

'But what exactly did your grandfather tell you?' asked a rather anxious Annie, who was becoming increasingly concerned about her worried parents.

'Well,' recollected Geoffrey, 'from what I can remember it's like time stands still and when the enchantment lifts and whoever or whatever returns to their normal size, only seconds will have gone by. So you see, your parents will still be on their way up to the top of Whernside when you go back outside as your usual size.'

The girls seemed to need a few moments to take in this new bit of information. Geoffrey wondered if they knew what each other was thinking. He watched their faces intently, trying to guess what they would say next. However, he was aware that for him time was moving on and he really needed to get to Jasper's. If only his grandfather had told him an enchantment to erase people's memories, that would have solved this problem once and for all. Unfortunately he hadn't, and Geoffrey was no nearer being able to think of a solution himself.

Chapter Ten

When Jonathan came round he was back in the cave, slumped against the cold damp walls. He shivered. His head felt strange, in fact his whole body felt as though it didn't belong to him. He lifted his hand up to his head, his arm felt like a lead weight. He looked around him but the light was fading and he found it difficult to see. He tried to remember what he was doing there, but he just couldn't seem to recall anything very clearly. Everything was just a blur. He knew he'd been to Thorpe Cloud, but then what happened? His thoughts were broken by a rough voice shouting at him.

'About time too,' yelled Freddy. 'I thought you'd never wake up. We haven't got long, you know. Now have some of that food of yours. You are going to need all your energy for what you've got to do tonight.' Freddy strode up closer to Jonathan so he could see him more clearly. The boy was pale, with glazed eyes. He looked like a feeble specimen of a human, shivering in the dimming light. How on earth was he supposed to carry out this mission successfully with this child? What a joke!

Without a second thought Jonathan reached for his rucksack and delved inside for some food. He ate some roast potatoes, chicken and an apple. After a few slugs of water he zipped up his bag once more. The whole scenario was so automated, as if a robot had acted it out. He glared into Freddy's bright green eyes, waiting for the next instruction.

Freddy was somewhat taken aback by the obedience shown by Jonathan. Axon had obviously had quite an effect on him. Perhaps this mission had a hope of succeeding after all.

'It's time to start moving,' said Freddy. 'The walkers should have finished for the day so we ought to be quite safe.'

Jonathan gazed up at Freddy, making no attempt to move. Freddy realised Jonathan was going to need precise instructions every step of the way. Axon had put him under some kind of spell, hopefully enabling Freddy to dictate every move to him without any chance of probing questions.

'Put your rucksack on and let's get moving,' Freddy ordered sternly.

Jonathan obeyed and they were ready to go. They walked back out through the arch and down the steep path. Jonathan was much more surefooted on the way down than he had been on the way up. He just marched on, not giving a second thought to where he was putting his feet. Stones scattered as he walked and he slipped a couple of times, but none of this was reflected in Jonathan's face. He just looked straight ahead and said nothing.

When they reached the main path by the river they turned right. Stretches of the narrow path were covered with wooden boards, but after a while the path opened back out onto a gravel track.

As they turned the corner, there it was; the face of a lion looking down into the river. There was still enough light to make out its features. Its face looked kind with its mouth firmly shut. There was nothing menacing about it, so perhaps whatever Freddy was going to ask Jonathan to do would not be so bad after all.

Freddy was looking around him, tilting his head from side

to side as if trying to listen for something.

'There is no one around now; it's safe to start the climb.'

Jonathan wavered. 'Climb? You don't seriously expect me to climb up onto the Lion's Head, do you?'

'That is precisely what we are both going to do. When we are inside I will need you to get the casket from where it is buried. That's something I can't do and I need your strength to do it for me.'

Jonathan knew that Ilam Rock was just a couple of minutes' walk further up the path. There was a bridge across the river. Should he make a run for it? In order to get back to Ilam he needed to be on the other side of the river. Would he be able to find his way back from there? It was risky, but surely worth a try.

'There's no way...' Jonathan's voice trailed off as Freddy's eyes bore into him. The green bulges glared with such ferocity that it seemed to wipe out all of Jonathan's self-will.

'You will do exactly as I say,' Freddy yelled menacingly.

Freddy led Jonathan to the little path by the side of the Lion's Head. There were a few trees growing close to the side of the rock, Freddy studied them carefully and then turned to Jonathan.

'Take off your rucksack; you won't be able to climb up there with that on your back.'

Jonathan meekly obeyed and set his rucksack down by the base of one of the trees. He was already trembling with trepidation and yet, although he should have been able to turn away and make his way back to Ilam, something was stopping him.

It was as if he was not in control of his own actions and he had no choice but to obey Freddy.

'Now you need to listen very carefully.' Freddy spoke more calmly now and there was a real sense of purpose coming through his voice that made Jonathan give him his full attention.

'We are going to climb up this tree and go across to the eye. There are plenty of places on the rock to grab hold of. Once we are by the eye you will see our way in. It will be best for me to sit on your shoulder so I can direct you to the precise place. Lift me up now and let's get going.'

Jonathan bent down and lifted Freddy onto his shoulder. Freddy held on to the collar of Jonathan's coat and once more looked up at the trees.

'This is the closest to the rock.' Freddy pointed to a rather spindly looking tree right beside them. As Jonathan looked at it his immediate thought was there was no way it would hold his weight. He had climbed many of the trees at Casterne Hall when he had been allowed to play in the grounds. But they had all been big sturdy specimens, with large branches and solid wide trunks. However, despite not wanting to attempt this climb, he found himself reaching up for the first branch and finding a foothold. Jonathan's previous tree climbing experiences stood him in good stead and although the tree was extremely shaky, he managed to climb up fairly easily. The branches were so thin he wasted no time in getting up as fast as he could, so as not to linger

too long on each one in case it snapped under his weight. When he was almost level with the Lion's eye he soon realised that climbing up the tree had been the easy part. There was a gap between the tree and the rock and he would have to swing from the branch in order to have any chance of landing safely. Then there was the question of where to land. Although there were places to grab hold of, one wrong move and that would be it.

Jonathan glanced down and suddenly lost his nerve. His thoughts flashed back to Mrs Milson and he felt all the love and kindness she had shown him over the years. Tears filled his eyes; he was so frightened now and didn't know which way to move. His fear of falling had made him freeze and panic began to rise inside him. He felt cold and clammy. He started to speak to Freddy to let him know he couldn't go on, but his throat was so dry not a sound came out.

'Why have you stopped?' yelled Freddy. 'We can't hang around here. Swing over and grab onto that bit jutting out. Can you see it? There is a little ledge underneath where you can put your feet.'

Jonathan remained motionless. Freddy sighed and realised a more forceful approach was needed again. Carefully, he reached for the front of Jonathan's coat and pulled himself around. Now he could see Jonathan's pale face and he knew he had to act quickly and decisively.

'Jonathan, look at me,' Freddy shouted. Jonathan looked down at Freddy and became transfixed on his green bulging eyes. They bore right into him as they had done before and Jonathan was once again under his power. Unbeknown to either of them, a black wispy cloud was hovering high above, waiting to intervene if necessary. But Freddy had regained control and Jonathan was preparing to move.

'Swing out now,' roared Freddy. Jonathan moved so abruptly Freddy nearly lost his hold. As Jonathan swung out and clasped his hand round a bit of the rock, he smacked hard into the surface, banging Freddy harshly against it. Jonathan's legs were dangling and he frantically moved them around to try and find a foothold. His grip was beginning to loosen and just as he thought he would fall, his toes touched something flat and he was able to put the tips of both his shoes onto the tiny ledge.

'Urrgh,' moaned Freddy, holding his hand to his head. Jonathan looked down to see a trickle of blood running down the side of Freddy's face.

'Oh, I'm so sorry,' Jonathan gasped. 'Are you alright?'

'Well I would have been had you not slammed me against the rock, you fool. Look what you've done; you could have knocked me out and then what would have happened. You need me you know.' Freddy was understandably a bit distraught and Jonathan knew it was pointless trying to apologise again. After all he hadn't hurt him on purpose. If Freddy had stayed on his shoulder instead of moving around to his chest none of this would have happened.

Jonathan looked down again as Freddy was mumbling some incomprehensible words. At first he thought he must have concussion, but then his eyes were drawn to the Lion's eye where something unbelievable was happening. Very slowly an opening appeared; it was like the eye was being slid apart. Jonathan was speechless; he could hardly grasp what was happening.

'Quick,' yelled Freddy, 'reach up and climb through the gap.'

Jonathan carefully stretched out his right arm but he

couldn't quite reach the bottom of the gap.

'I can't reach. It's too high.'

'You will just have to jump up then, and make sure you don't miss,' Freddy replied gruffly. 'Now get on with it. JUMP!'

Jonathan hesitated. This was madness. He only had one chance and if he messed up he would certainly die.

'JUMP!' hollered Freddy impatiently.

Jonathan took a deep breath, pushed hard down on his toes and leapt upwards with both arms outstretched. His fingers grabbed onto the surface at the base of the opening and steadily he pulled himself up into the gap.

Chapter Eleven

Jonathan found himself gazing into a large cavern. Water trickled down the stone walls and clumps of moss lay between some of the crevices. The walls looked so pretty, with their different shades of orange, beige, green and grey. A loud creaking noise was coming from behind him and as he turned he saw the gap that had magically appeared in the Lion's eye was slowly closing.

'Move forward and put me down,' ordered Freddy.

Jonathan did as he was told. As the gap closed, the cavern began to look very dim and soon it was very difficult to see ahead. He wished he had brought the torch that was in his rucksack.

'Stand still for a moment and your eyes will soon adjust,' reassured Freddy briskly.

Jonathan waited and sure enough he began to make out the outline to the cave again. Ahead, he could see a streak of light shining down from the corner and in the distance he could hear the faint sound of water trickling along. As he looked up he saw rows of sparkling lights and as he stopped and studied them he realised it was a colony of glow-worms. There had been a book about them in the school library that he had looked through. He had read about the surveys that had been conducted to keep a track of where the glow-worms were as their colonies were under threat. Of course, this was one colony that would never be seen, but there had been a single female seen many years ago near the stepping stones he had crossed last night on his way to Thorpe Cloud. He wondered if they were somehow connected.

'Follow me,' demanded Freddy, 'and be careful where you put your feet. It's very uneven in places.'

Jonathan was brought abruptly away from his thoughts and he followed closely behind Freddy as he moved cautiously towards the back of the cave. The ground was certainly uneven, with large potholes in places where you could easily twist an ankle if you weren't looking where you were going. Freddy stopped suddenly as he reached a large boulder, a few feet from the far corner where the light was flickering down.

'This is the place,' he said excitedly. 'Now, all you have to do is move this boulder out of the way.'

'What's underneath it that's so important?' Jonathan asked. He was beginning to get some of his confidence back and was curious to know why Freddy had gone to so much trouble to get here. It was obviously something very special to risk his life for.

'Just do as I say,' yelled Freddy. 'The sooner we get this done the sooner we can be out of here and you can be on your way back to Ilam. Now, stop asking so many questions. You will see soon enough.'

Jonathan was about to protest but he could clearly see that Freddy was obviously not going to give in, so he bent down and knelt by the boulder. It was bigger than he had first thought, reaching up to above his waist as he knelt beside it. It was too wide to get his arms completely round it, so he placed them as far around as he could and tried to move it towards him. It didn't even shift an inch. This was going to be harder than he thought. He tried various positions, bending over it, pulling, pushing with his legs and then his arms, but nothing was working. He sat down to get his breath back. He had been putting so much energy into trying to move the boulder he was suddenly exhausted.

'Don't just sit there you lazy boy. Keep trying.' Freddy was becoming very impatient and not at all sympathetic to Jonathan's physical state.

Jonathan knelt up again and this time tried to rock the boulder backwards and forwards. It moved very slightly and Jonathan began to rock it once more as vigorously as he could. Gradually, the boulder moved to reveal a large hole underneath.

Freddy was jumping up and down in excitement. 'You've done it, you've done it,' he shrieked. 'Move out of the way and let me see.'

Jonathan sat down and swung his legs away from the hole. Freddy peered in but it was too dark to make out anything. A cold breeze came up from the hole and the sound of trickling water grew louder.

'I know it's down there, I just can't see it,' mumbled Freddy frustratingly.

'Well if you told me what to look for maybe I could reach down and see if I can feel it,' said Jonathan, beginning to feel more and more exasperated by the whole situation.

Freddy looked across and was about to snap back at him when he thought better of it. The boy had a point; after all, he wasn't going to be able to get the casket by himself.

'Very well,' said Freddy. 'It's a square casket about 2cm in diameter.'

'That small, but surely…'

'Of course it's small,' interrupted Freddy. 'How else do

you think a Trignome could carry it?'

'Oh, I hadn't really thought about that,' replied Jonathan meekly. 'What's in it?'

'Never you mind, just stick your hand down there and carefully feel around.'

'No,' said Jonathan, 'not until you tell me what's in it.'

Freddy was taken aback by this sudden assertive tone from Jonathan. He glared at him, but Jonathan didn't flinch or succumb to his power. He continued to just sit and stare at him defiantly.

Jonathan noticed that Freddy's eyes were no longer a bright green, but were gradually reverting back to black. The hold that Freddy had on him was gone and he realised that Freddy was losing this strange power that had taken over him. Freddy was visibly crumbling back into the nervous creature he had first met at the top of Lover's Leap after he had freed him from the rock.

For a few moments there was a stunned silence between them and then awkwardness crept in as Freddy tried to pull himself back together. He was in such a fluster that he couldn't get his words out right and he wasn't making any sense. Jonathan looked at him, bemused by the whole affair. As Freddy caught sight of this look he knew he owed this poor child a thorough explanation.

'I'm, I'm so very sorry,' he stammered. 'I don't know how to begin to explain what has been happening. You need to know that I never meant you any harm. It just wasn't me you see, it was… oh, how can I make it all clear to you?' Freddy sat down with his head in his hands, at a complete loss as to where to start and how to put things right.

Jonathan moved to sit beside him and gently put his hand

on his shoulder. 'Why don't you start by explaining why you changed so much? Your eyes went green and you were so aggressive and mean.'

'It was Axon,' Freddy said quietly. 'He has no power underground or in any enclosed space. His enchantment has worn off and he can't get to us whilst we are here.'

'But who is Axon?' asked Jonathan.

'About forty years ago there was a Trignome who came from over the sea. It was never clear exactly where he had come from. There were lots of rumours, of course. Most thought he came from Russia or one of the countries that previously formed part of the Russian Empire. This was the only area where they knew other Trignomes lived. The Russian trig points were much bigger, more like monuments, but Trignomes lived in them just the same. At first, this stranger tried to befriend as many Trignomes as he could, winning them over with his swashbuckling stories of adventure and filling them with admiration. He travelled all over the country and his stories spread far and wide. Whoever he visited welcomed him into their home unreservedly and he grew accustomed to being treated like a hero. That was until he met Rowena.'

Freddy paused and looked up at Jonathan, his face full of sadness. Jonathan waited patiently for Freddy to continue.

'Rowena lived with her brother on Pen-y-ghent, one of the three peaks in the Yorkshire Dales. When the Trignome arrived, Rowena's brother, Thomas, was so excited and totally taken in by his charm and stories of bravery. Rowena on the other hand, was not. She was older than Thomas and very protective of her younger brother. She didn't like the way Thomas hung on every word this strange Trignome uttered and how he pampered to his every need. The stranger's name was

Axon and he clearly loved being the centre of attention. However, there was something about him that made Rowena feel uneasy. He was very pleasant to look at; taller than any gnome she had met before, with thick set shoulders and a mop of black tight curly hair. His skin was tanned, but there was something about his green eyes that made her shudder when she looked into them. It was as if there was something untrustworthy about him. He spoke with a very rough, yet somehow haunting accent. She tried to ask him more probing questions about where he had come from and what had happened to his family. Still, as hard as she tried, she never got a straight answer and this troubled her.

Normally Axon only stayed a few days and then moved on. This time was different though. Rowena was a very beautiful Trignome with long flowing red hair and large hazel eyes. There was something so enchanting about her that Axon didn't want to leave. Her grovelling little brother was becoming quite irritating, but he was happy to put up with that just so he could stay near her. Whenever Rowena tried to talk to Thomas about asking Axon to leave, he wouldn't hear of it and was completely oblivious to the longing looks Axon was directing at his sister.'

Freddy paused again and sighed, as if needing a moment to collect his thoughts. 'It was a tragedy waiting to happen and yet no one saw it coming, although perhaps Rowena was the most aware of all. Axon made his feelings for her clear, but she rebuffed him time and time again. Thomas couldn't understand why Rowena was behaving so rudely to their guest and told her how lucky she was to have such a fine admirer. After another few days of persistent pressure from both Thomas and Axon, Rowena decided to stand up for herself and say how she really felt. To the astonishment of Thomas, she told Axon in no uncertain terms exactly what she thought of him and asked him to leave her home immediately. Axon had not experienced anything like this since he came to Britain and it filled him with rage. He raised his hand to Rowena, knocking her to the ground. Again and again he hit her and as Thomas tried to intervene, he was knocked unconscious. When Thomas came round, he found Rowena lying dead by his side. Heartbroken and full of guilt for not listening to his sister, he vowed he would track Axon down and kill him.

Months passed as Thomas searched for Axon. News of his plight spread across the country and other Trignomes joined him in his search for justice. Then at last Thomas found him. He'd been told that Axon was spotted back on Pen-y ghent and he had been using the trig point for shelter. This infuriated Thomas even more and he headed back to deal with him alone. However, when he arrived there something was not right. He could sense an atmosphere that he did not recognise and as he opened the door to enter, a strange smell wafted out at him. Thomas crept in, trying not to make a sound. He realised the smell was coming from a pan on the stove which was bubbling away. Axon was nowhere to be seen. As he turned the corner and looked towards the bedroom he saw that Axon was asleep on the bed.'

Again Freddy paused. It was clear to Jonathan that he was finding this particular part of the story difficult to relate. He looked up at Jonathan with great sorrow in his eyes and then carried on, knowing he had to finish the tale, however painful it was to tell it.

'Until this moment Thomas had not thought about what he would do when he found Axon. You see, Trignomes are not violent by nature. They are caring folk who go about their daily lives with only goodness in their hearts. They are always willing to help other Trignomes who may be in need, no matter what the cost to them. That is just the way they are. So when he saw Axon lying there, although filled with hate and anger, his instinct was stopping him from committing a violent act. Still, events took over as at that very moment Axon woke up and saw Thomas standing, motionless.

As quick as a flash he was off the bed and heading towards Thomas. His face was contorted with anger and he was laughing with the most horrible evil cackle imaginable. Without a second thought Thomas reached backwards and felt for the pan handle. With a quick flick of the wrist he threw the contents at Axon. In the split second before the liquid reached him, Thomas saw the look of horror across his face. Axon raised up his arms, but it was too late. As the liquid landed on him he let out a terrifying scream. It splattered across his chest and face and Thomas watched in disbelief as Axon disappeared before his eyes. A black wispy cloud hovered over where he had been standing and then it was gone. Only Thomas was left; shocked and shaken about what had just happened.'

'The black wispy cloud?' asked Jonathan. 'Is that Axon?'

'Yes,' Freddy replied solemnly.

'I remember it when I tried to leave Reynard's Cave. It suddenly came down over me and then I don't remember what happened after that.'

Chapter Twelve

They both sat in silence, as if in their own little worlds with their private thoughts. Jonathan sat and mulled over all that Freddy had told him. There was so much to take in and so many questions going through his mind. He was trying to make sense of it all, but it was like trying to do a jigsaw with pieces missing.

'How do you know so much about what happened with Axon, and what has the casket got to do with it all?'

'Rowena was my aunty,' Freddy replied quietly.

'So Thomas is your father,' said Jonathan incredulously.

'Yes, that's right,' Freddy mumbled. 'It took him a good few years to get over what had happened to Rowena, but eventually he started to get out and about more and he met my mum. They live on Pen-y-ghent with my younger sister. I didn't know all the details about what had happened until a few weeks ago. Of course, I knew that Aunty Rowena had died when she was young, but that was all. Then one afternoon Dad came back from berry picking and his face was ashen. Mum seemed to know something terrible had happened and she ushered my sister and I outside to collect some leaves. I happened to be visiting for a few days and couldn't understand what all the secrecy was about. After what seemed like an eternity, Mum called us back in. Dad was sat in the armchair with his head in his hands. He looked up as we walked in and asked us to sit down. Mum stood behind him with her hand on his shoulder. She'd obviously been crying as her eyes were red and swollen, but she managed a reassuring smile as she looked into our anxious faces.

She told us that Dad had got something very important to tell us and it was clear from her voice that she was very apprehensive about it. That's when I discovered the truth about what had happened all those years before. Dad told us everything, just as I told you. The problem was, Axon was back, or rather he was back in a different form. Dad had not seen him since the day he had attacked him with the contents of the pan. He'd heard rumours, of course. He'd told a few friends about what had happened and word spread as it does, especially as so many Trignomes had met Axon and thought he was some sort of hero. That was until he killed Rowena and then there wasn't a Trignome in the land who would have taken him in. There were various sightings of a black wispy cloud seen hovering around several trig points in the country. Some Trignomes reckoned they had felt it wrapped around them, as if trying to take over their mind. As it happens, it sounds as though those stories were true.'

'What do you mean?' asked Jonathan.

'Well,' continued Freddy, 'when Dad had been berry picking, the black wispy cloud appeared over him. It made him go into some sort of trance and when Dad got hold of his senses again he realised that he had had a conversation with Axon. Dad said that Axon had explained that the potion he had been mixing when Dad found him on Pen-y-ghent wasn't complete and that's why he had been turned into a cloud. Now he wanted Dad to help him become a Trignome again.'

'Has the casket that's down there got something to do with this?' Jonathan asked as he peered down the hole.

'It certainly has,' sighed Freddy. 'Dad told us that Axon had been mixing the magical potion to use on him to change him into a different creature. It was a sort of punishment for trying to hunt Axon down. Dad, of course, had no idea what it was and the effect it had on Axon took them both by surprise. Axon spent many years trying to find a remedy that would reverse the effects of the potion. He travelled far and wide only to find out that the answer lay right here.

Apparently, Axon's uncle had visited this country after he had gone missing. It was probably the same person who had taught Axon about potions in the first place. He managed to gather information about what had happened from various Trignomes and he set about making the remedy and hiding it somewhere where Axon could get to it. That proved more difficult than he thought. He made the casket but didn't know what to do with it. Somehow he heard about the Lion's Head and knew if he could get a message to Axon, it would be a very safe place to store the remedy. No one would ever find it there. He painted some sort of magic potion onto the rock that seeped into the eye. That's how we managed to get in. Axon's uncle is certainly a very clever magician.'

'But how did he get the message to Axon?' asked Jonathan. 'Surely that must have been very difficult.'

'Seemingly not.' Freddy smiled to himself; luck had played its part. 'The uncle heard that Axon had been spotted nearby so he went to look for him. Sure enough, they found each other and that's when the information was passed on. Unfortunately, when the casket had been placed in the cave of the Lion's Head there had been an earth tremor and a boulder had fallen and covered the hole. Now the task to retrieve the casket had become far more difficult. For some reason, none of the uncle's powers worked inside the cave, so he had been unable to move it. The remedy had taken months and months to prepare so there was only one solution to the problem. Someone stronger than a Trignome had to get into the cave and retrieve the casket.'

'Lucky for you I came to the rescue,' said Jonathan with a smile on his face. 'What I don't understand is how you ended up under Axon's spell?'

'Simple really,' replied Freddy. 'Axon had been trying to get into the minds of Trignomes for years without success. Then, when he met his uncle, he told him that he would only be able to communicate with my dad or his blood relative. He had to follow the link between them, as Dad had been the one to throw the potion. When Axon approached Dad and told him what had to be done, he of course, said no. That's when Axon went crazy and said he would kill us all if he didn't do as he was told. When Dad told us what had happened I knew he would never be able to carry out the mission. He's quite frail now, you see, and never travels far. The only solution was for me to take on the task.

Mum and Dad were dead against it at first, but they soon realised we had no choice, not if we wanted to live. So Dad agreed and handed me over to Axon. The strange thing is that Axon's power over me only lasts a short time, so every now and again he would come back and turn me into his evil little puppet again.'

'I see,' said Jonathan. 'So when you were caught under the rock, the spell he had you under had worn off.'

'Precisely. It wasn't until you had told me your story that he came back and once again I was under his control. I don't think he'd thought about how we were going to find someone to help move the boulder in the cave, but you happened to come along just at the right time.'

Jonathan nodded. 'When I wouldn't cooperate anymore Axon somehow managed to put me under his spell too.' Now he understood. The jigsaw was complete. Or was it?

'So he will be waiting for us when we get back outside I presume.'

'Absolutely, and there's no guarantee what he will do to us once he is changed back. The main problem is that no Trignome has ever revealed themselves to humans before. You know too much and that could endanger the lives of all Trignomes.'

'But I would never do anything to hurt you or any Trignome,' Jonathan protested. 'I can keep a secret – that's a promise.'

'I'm sure you can.' Freddy patted Jonathan gently on the leg. 'If it was up to me I wouldn't be worried. I know you are an honourable boy who has shown great courage. Axon, however, is a different matter. He has no mercy; we have to think of a way to make it safe for you. Do you fancy trying to get the casket whilst we are thinking?'

Jonathan smiled warmly at Freddy. As Freddy looked back at him Jonathan could see worry and regret in his eyes. He thought for a moment how hard it must be for Freddy now. He realised Freddy felt responsible for getting him into this situation, but strangely, all Jonathan could do was be concerned for Freddy and his family; he hadn't given a thought to the danger he was in himself.

'I think I can feel something,' Jonathan shouted excitedly. Freddy turned to see Jonathan's legs stretched along the edge of the hole; the rest of his body wasn't visible.

'Be careful,' yelled Freddy. 'You could fall in!'

'I've nearly got it; just a bit further.' Jonathan wriggled deeper into the hole and just as Freddy thought he would surely fall in, his body slowly emerged. In his hand he held the tiny casket.

'Got it!' Jonathan smiled at Freddy triumphantly. They both gazed at the casket for a few seconds and then Freddy held out his hands.

'May I take a look?' he asked.

'Of course,' said Jonathan as he handed it over.

Freddy examined the casket carefully. It was made of wood; ash he thought. What puzzled him was how to get into it. It looked like it was completely sealed with no sign of an opening. Then, as he turned it on its side, he saw a tiny clasp indented so discreetly into the grain of the wood it was hardly noticeable. Cautiously, he released it and the casket slowly opened to reveal a small glass vial carefully embedded in sand.

'What now?' asked Jonathan as he peered into the casket. 'How are we going to deal with Axon?'

'We have to have a plan,' said Freddy seriously. 'Once he has been changed back into a Trignome, who knows what he will do.'

'Perhaps we could trick him and not let him change back.' Jonathan scratched his head, trying hard to think of what they could do. Both of them remained silent for a few minutes, so deep in thought that neither seemed aware of the other.

Jonathan yawned and rubbed his eyes, he suddenly felt completely drained. 'You poor boy, you must be exhausted,' Freddy said softly. 'Let's nestle down here for the night and we can sleep on it. We can think again in the morning when our heads are clearer.'

Without his rucksack Jonathan had no blanket to wrap around him. It was cold in the cave but he knew he would just have to make the best of it. He lay down on the hard floor and Freddy snuggled beside him. They were both soon asleep despite the cold, damp conditions; they were too weary to care. They slept for several hours until Freddy broke the silence.

'I think I've got it!' he shouted excitedly.

Jonathan woke up with a start and took a few moments to remember where he was. His body felt stiff and he ached all over.

'The only problem is, we need more of us to make it work.' Freddy was fumbling about under his coat when he produced a whistle from his trouser pocket.

'What good will that do?' asked Jonathan sleepily. 'It's just a whistle.'

'This isn't any old whistle,' Freddy explained. 'We all carry one with us when we are journeying away from home. It is only to be used in emergencies, but if a Trignome is in trouble and needs help, then blowing on this whistle will send a message to another Trignome and they will come to our assistance. I reckon it's early morning so someone is bound to be out and about. The only trouble is once one Trignome has picked up the message, that's it. No one else will be able to hear it and we could do with a whole army. If we could cause some sort of commotion and entice Axon into the Lion's Head we could then trap him inside, close the rock and he would be entombed forever. His powers can't work in here so he would have no way of escaping.'

'Ingenious!' shouted Jonathan. 'Then we would both be safe and your family too.'

'Yes, that's true, but I'm not sure we can succeed with

only a little help. It's a shame we aren't able to call on your friends, then we would definitely have a chance of success. Still, that's not possible so let's see who the whistle brings.'

Freddy walked towards the back corner of the cave, where the streak of light was shining through.

'Hopefully the sound will travel through this crack.' He raised the whistle to his lips and gave a long hard blow. As he did so he closed his eyes and sent his wordless message, so the Trignome who picked up his signal would understand and know exactly where to find him.

Chapter Thirteen

'How old are you two?' asked Geoffrey.

'Eight,' replied the twins together. They looked at each other and smiled, that sort of thing happened a lot. Someone would ask a question and they would both answer at exactly the same time, in exactly the same way.

'Look, I'm in a bit of a predicament,' Geoffrey continued. 'As I mentioned earlier, no human has ever seen a Trignome before and if anyone else were to find out that we existed; well, there is no knowing what might become of us. Can eight-year-olds keep such a big secret?'

Lizzie and Annie looked at each other again and hesitated.

'Well, it's not good to keep secrets, particularly from our parents,' replied Annie.

'Yes, but this is different Annie,' said Lizzie. 'We can't let anything awful happen to Geoffrey and his friends. I think on this occasion it's ok to keep this secret. There's just one thing Geoffrey. What's a predicament?'

Geoffrey smiled. 'It's a dilemma, not knowing what to do for the best. It's like having a problem and not knowing how to solve it. You know we exist now so I can't wipe that from your minds, so I have to be sure you will keep the secret, otherwise I may have led all Trignomes into great danger.'

'Don't worry, you will be quite safe,' Annie reassured him. 'We will keep your secret, we promise. We would never want anyone to harm you.'

'Thank you,' sighed Geoffrey. 'You certainly are two very special girls and I will always remember you. But now I have to be on my way and I need to return you back to your normal size.'

'Yes, of course, and thank you so much for showing us your lovely home,' Lizzie mumbled softly. She didn't want this to come to an end, but she knew it had to be that way. She bent down and grabbed hold of Elsa's collar.

'Come on Elsa, time to go.' They moved slowly towards the door, Geoffrey in front and Annie trailing at the rear. She turned and had one last look around before going out onto the hillside once more.

'Right, we need to hold hands in a circle again. Once I have spoken the enchantment you will be back to your normal size and I will have to leave very quickly. Your parents will be here within moments. Lizzie, please make sure you don't let go of Elsa, not until I'm safely in the air.'

Before Lizzie got a chance to respond, Elsa let out a long sorrowful whine. Geoffrey let go of the girls and put his hands to his head, closed his eyes and stood motionless for a few seconds. The girls looked at each other, but seemed to sense not to speak. They waited for him to open his eyes again. Meanwhile, Elsa had stopped howling and stood patiently, like she was anticipating something else was about to happen.

'Someone's in trouble and needs our help.' Geoffrey sounded extremely concerned. 'There's no time to explain, I can tell you on the way. Will you do it? Will you come with me?'

'But Mum and Dad,' whispered Annie.

'It's all right, Annie. Remember what Geoffrey told us.

Time is different whilst we are still small. They won't know we have gone anywhere. That's true isn't it, Geoffrey?'

'Yes, Lizzie, that's right, but we have to hurry. Will you come? I wouldn't ask if I didn't need you.'

'Of course we'll come.' Lizzie looked reassuringly at Annie and she nodded slowly.

Geoffrey hid his backpack behind a stone in the wall. He quickly walked towards the grass and ripped out a few big chunks. Carefully he separated out some of the blades of grass and waved his hands over them.

'Whakakaha, whakakaha,' he uttered. He then proceeded to tie the blades of grass together until he had what looked like a long rope. He rushed back to the girls and Elsa.

'Do up your coats,' he said. 'I'm going to tie us all together with this grass so you will be safe.'

'Grass?' queried Annie. 'What good will that do? Surely it will just break.'

'I have just cast an enchantment over it to strengthen it; feel it.' Geoffrey offered the line of grass to Annie. Sure enough, as she pulled on it as hard as she could, it held together, as strong as steel. Geoffrey carefully wrapped the grass around himself and then the girls. Securing Elsa was proving to be more difficult, but eventually he managed to link the grass through her collar and under her tummy and lastly join it back to himself.

'Ok,' he said rather apprehensively. 'Are you ready?' The girls nodded, not really knowing what to expect.

'Rere atu,' Geoffrey called. 'Hold on tight, and Lizzie hang on to Elsa's collar. Off we go!'

They were suddenly lifted into the air, Geoffrey at the front and Lizzie, Annie and Elsa bundled together behind him.

Lizzie had to shout firmly at Elsa to stop her barking, whilst Annie looked absolutely petrified.

'It's ok,' yelled Lizzie to Annie, 'just try and relax. This is amazing!'

They travelled quite high in the sky so it was very difficult to make out what was beneath them. The girls' blonde hair was lifting and swirling in the wind like the mane of a galloping horse. They could see matchbox towns and villages and vast areas of open countryside. Annie soon relaxed and both the girls began to enjoy the experience. It was almost impossible to talk with the wind roaring in their ears, rushing them along at a fair pace. Geoffrey started to explain where they were going but they could only make out a muffled sound. When they tried to speak, the air seemed to get caught in their throat, so they soon settled down to an accepted silence, each thinking their own thoughts. Despite the strength of the wind it felt like they were just gliding through the sky, like the clouds gently moving across on a summer's day. Even Elsa seemed to be resigned to endure the journey and was nestled under Lizzie's arm.

It was difficult to say how long they had been flying through the sky, but after a while it was obvious they were heading downwards, closer to land. The girls could make out little black and white dots in the green fields below, which they soon realised were cows and sheep. They could also now see miniature stone cottages and the grey stone walls that edged the green fields. As they veered to the right a long meandering river came into view, with steep banks of limestone interspersed with trees encroaching on each side.

Geoffrey signalled by repeatedly pointing his finger downwards. Lizzie and Annie nodded, showing him they had understood. Geoffrey seemed hesitant, as if he wasn't quite sure where to land. They could sense his tension, as his whole body seemed to have stiffened.

They were now flying much lower and were just above the limestone cliffs and the river. They dropped even more and suddenly it looked like they were heading straight for what looked like a finger pointing up towards the sky from the tree line.

'Look out!' shouted Lizzie and Annie simultaneously.

Geoffrey veered quickly to the left and they all landed with a thump at the base of Ilam rock. Luckily for them the ground was covered with thick grass and moss so the landing was somewhat cushioned.

'Sorry about that, I don't normally land that badly. Are you all right?'

'Yes thank you,' replied Lizzie. 'Annie, are you ok?'

Annie looked a little shaken, but she nodded and smiled. Lizzie was the eldest of the two by fifteen minutes and she had always taken on the older sister role. She was more confident than Annie and usually took the lead in anything they did together. Elsa let out a little bark as if to let them know she was all right too! The girls looked at her and smiled. Geoffrey untied them and carefully placed the line of grass in his coat pocket. He knew he would need that for their return journey.

'Now I need to explain to you what has happened,' said Geoffrey solemnly.

Chapter Fourteen

The girls sat and listened as Geoffrey told them all he knew about Freddy and Jonathan's situation. Freddy was a few years older than Geoffrey and he had known him all his life. In fact, as a young Trignome he had often played with Freddy and his younger sister. Their trig points were only a few miles apart. Once Freddy moved to Ecton Hill they didn't see very much of each other, but he was a good Trignome and Geoffrey was only too happy to help him. However, from the brief message he had got from Freddy, it all sounded rather bizarre.

He had heard of Axon's fate, as most Trignomes had, but he had no idea that he had such power. The fact that there was a boy involved made the whole situation far more complicated, although in some ways it was comforting to know that he was not the only Trignome to reveal himself to humans. It was because of the boy that he had wanted to bring Lizzie and Annie along. It was just an instinctive feeling he had. Perhaps somehow they could help the situation in a way he could not.

Lizzie and Annie were staring at each other in disbelief. They had recognised Ilam Rock as they landed. They had seen it many times as they had often walked along the river with their mum and aunty. It was a well-known landmark in the area as it looked like a finger pointing up to the sky. They knew exactly where they were.

'You two look like you have seen a ghost,' said Geoffrey, startled.

'Well, it's just that we may know Jonathan,' Lizzie began slowly.

Geoffrey's jaw dropped open in disbelief. He was about to speak when Lizzie explained.

'We are in Dovedale which is just a couple of miles from Ilam where our aunty and uncle live. In fact, we are visiting them in a few days. We often spend time here and have become very good friends with a boy called Jonathan. It may be just a coincidence; after all, there could easily be other boys in the area with the same name.'

'That is interesting,' mused Geoffrey. 'Still, it doesn't alter anything. Whether you know him or not, it's still going to be a very difficult rescue.'

'Do you have a plan?' Lizzie asked expectantly.

'Well,' Geoffrey hesitated. 'To be perfectly honest I'm not quite sure how to go about this. It's not very straightforward. Let's walk across to the Lion's Head and assess the situation there.'

They walked across the footbridge with Elsa following obediently by their side. She had wanted to go into the river as she loved water, but Annie had told her firmly, 'no'. Annie knew that being so tiny meant Elsa would not have the strength to swim against the flow of the river and she could easily be washed downstream.

When they had crossed over the bridge, Geoffrey pointed up the path. 'There it is.'

The girls knew that once they had walked past the trees, they would be able to look back and see the face of the Lion. They had seen it before, of course, but it never ceased to fill them with wonder. It was such a gentle looking face. Geoffrey was about to march on when Annie stopped him.

'Hang on!' she said. 'What if this Axon thing is waiting outside the cave? Surely if he sees us he may get suspicious.'

'You're right,' Geoffrey sighed. 'I hadn't thought of that. I suppose he must have to sleep sometime though, just like the rest of us. You two wait here and I will creep along and see if there is any sign of him.'

Geoffrey walked quietly and steadily towards the Lion's Head, keeping close to the inner edge of the path. As he looked about him he could see no sign of a black wispy cloud. He gazed in amazement at the big rock above him, trying to figure out how a boy could have climbed up there safely. It was unbelievable. As he looked on he knew he had to think of a way to ensure the safety of the girls and Elsa. It was quite a risk they would all be taking and he couldn't allow anything to happen to them. He was brought back from his thoughts by a dog barking.

'Elsa,' he said to himself. Then it dawned on him, she was the answer. He rushed back to where the girls were waiting.

'It's ok,' he panted, 'Axon is nowhere to be seen, but we must hurry. He's going to turn up soon, I'm sure of it. Is Elsa a very obedient dog?'

'Most of the time,' Lizzie smiled. 'Why?'

'I think she may hold the trump card here. It's too dangerous for you two to climb up onto the rock and anyway, you will make a good distraction on the ground. Once the entrance into the cave is open you can start making a noise and that will divert Axon. If Elsa could scramble up to the eye, she could then attract Axon's attention and he will become very confused. She is now so small he won't be at all sure what sort of creature she is. He is bound to follow her if she enters the cave; Trignomes are naturally very curious folk. This will hopefully give Freddy and Jonathan enough time to get out, call Elsa back and close the entrance.'

'That sounds like a good plan, Geoffrey,' said Annie thoughtfully. 'But how will Freddy know that we are here?'

'He won't. There is no way we can communicate with him. He will just trust that someone picked up his message and will have come up with some sort of plan to help. I will climb up with Elsa and hope she is able to do as I say. I think we should make a move now and you two need to hide behind the trees until you can see Axon is by the open entrance. I don't think it will be long until he makes an appearance. He will be anxious to get hold of the potion. Any questions?'

'You will be very careful won't you?' Annie asked quietly, a small tear appearing in the corner of her eye.

Lizzie put her arm around her sister. 'We will be back on Whernside in no time, won't we Geoffrey?'

'Of course we will. Now, off you go and we will see each other again soon.' Geoffrey gave the girls a reassuring smile. They patted Elsa gently on the head and made their way slowly to the trees at the side of the rock.

Lizzie sensed Geoffrey was feeling uneasy and that he was not at all sure when they would be back at his trig point. So many things could go wrong. This whole situation was fraught with danger. Still, she knew he was going to do his very best. She heard him take in a deep breath.

'Come on, Elsa; good girl,' Geoffrey said gently. He started to scramble up the side of the rock with Elsa at his side. It wasn't easy, but being small sometimes had its advantages. There were lots of little hollows in the rock that made it easier to grab hold of the surface. They had soon reached the eye and they climbed just above the left hand corner to a little crevice shielded by a patch of hanging moss; ideal for them to hide behind. Geoffrey held on tightly to Elsa and hoped she would stay still. One quick jerk from her could send them both crashing to the ground below.

Geoffrey's hunch had been right, as it wasn't long before Axon appeared. A shadow was cast into the small crevice and as Geoffrey carefully peeped through a gap in the moss, he saw a black wispy cloud hovering in front of the Lion's left eye. Elsa began to let out a low growl as if she had sensed something bad was near. Quickly, Geoffrey whispered to her to be quiet and he held her closer. Never would he have imagined being this near to a dog before!

The cloud kept still for a while, but seemed to become increasingly impatient as he waited for Freddy to appear. It swirled around the rock making a faint whistling noise as it swept back and forth.

Chapter Fifteen

'I think we have left enough time now,' said Freddy, not sounding completely convinced. 'We need to get going.' He picked up the casket and placed it carefully inside his coat pocket.

'How do you know someone is here to help us?' asked Jonathan.

'We just have to trust that a Trignome heard the whistle. I expect Axon will be waiting for us outside the eye. He will want to get this potion as soon as he can. If no one is there to help we will somehow have to manage on our own. I will say the casket is stuck and we need a bit more time to get it out. Hopefully, Axon will want to look for himself and that way we can get to the entrance. It's not going to be easy for you to get back across to the tree safely. If there is help out there they can distract Axon, giving you more time to escape. Are you ready?'

'As ready as I'll ever be,' smiled Jonathan, trying hard not to show Freddy how scared he was.

'Once we are behind the eye, stand to the side. As soon as Axon moves in you need to get out. I think you probably need to jump straight across to the tree. It's not as far as it looks. Just give it all you have got and you will be fine.'

They both looked at each other, knowing how uncertain the next few moments were going to be. Freddy moved slowly towards the entrance to the cave and Jonathan followed behind.

They were nearly there when Jonathan let out a cry. He had been so focussed on getting to where the opening had been, he had forgotten to look where he was putting his feet. His right foot caught in a pothole and he tumbled to the ground. Freddy turned around abruptly.

'Are you alright?' he asked anxiously.

Jonathan tried to stand up but let out another cry.

'It's my ankle; I think I've sprained it. I can't seem to put any weight on it.' Freddy sighed not knowing what to do.

'I'm so sorry, maybe it will feel better in a minute.' Jonathan was finding it hard not to cry. It really hurt and he knew that his chances of escape now were very slim. He would never be able to push off and jump into the tree.

'Ok, let's wait a few minutes. Don't worry, we will think of something,' Freddy said gently. He could see Jonathan was in a lot of pain but he was powerless to help him. Their difference in size meant it was impossible for him to give Jonathan any support to walk. Jonathan leaned forward to undo his trainer.

'No,' shouted Freddy abruptly. 'If you have sprained it badly, your foot is going to start to swell up very quickly and you will never get your shoe on again. I'm not sure it's going to get any better, Jonathan. See if you can hop; you could still make it to the tree if you push off really hard on your left foot.'

Jonathan knew Freddy was right. It wasn't going to get any better in the short time they had. He got to his knees and pushed up on his left foot. As soon as he put any pressure on his right foot a sharp pain passed up through his leg. He bit his lip and tried not to let out another cry. Slowly, he hopped to the entrance, lunging forward to catch the wall for support.

'You know, once I have opened the Lion's eye there won't

be a moment to lose, especially now.' Freddy looked up at Jonathan once more. 'There is no other way out of this. I'm so very sorry to have put you in so much danger, but now it's up to you to get yourself out. You can do this.'

'Yes, I can. Don't worry Freddy, I'll make it. Just make sure you meet me at the bottom, having locked up that monster for good.'

'Sure thing,' smiled Freddy. 'See you at the bottom.' Freddy glanced at the wall of the cave and began to mumble. Slowly the wall began to move and a dim light penetrated through the gap. Freddy began to tremble as he saw the black wispy cloud circling outside. As soon as the cloud was still Freddy began to speak, explaining to Axon that the casket was stuck and they were having trouble retrieving it. The cloud swirled around so fast and caused such a gust of wind that Geoffrey nearly lost his balance from the crevice above.

Lizzie and Annie had been staring at the Lion's eye ever since they had hidden behind the trees. Now at last, they could see it slide open. They watched the black wispy cloud carefully and as it began to swirl again they started shouting below. The cloud moved down the rock swiftly, as if needing to take a closer look.

In this moment, Geoffrey turned to Elsa. He looked around him in horror; where was she? He glanced downwards and could just see her. She was almost as far down as the Lion's mouth and she was trying like mad to scramble back up the rock. When the cloud's swirling had nearly caused Geoffrey to lose his balance, Elsa must have slipped. This wasn't in the plan. He could see that Axon had nearly reached the girls and that was never meant to happen either. The whole idea was that Elsa would attract his attention before he got to them. Geoffrey was consumed with fear and panic. He was beside himself with concern for Lizzie and Annie's safety. He watched helplessly as the black wispy cloud encircled the two little figures below.

Chapter Sixteen

Lizzie and Annie hadn't seen Elsa fall as the cloud had obscured their view. Now they watched in dismay as it approached them. They were petrified, not sure what to do. Instinctively they started to run down the path but it was no good. The cloud soon enveloped them and they stood frozen to the spot, clinging to each other for support. The girls could almost feel the hesitation while Axon decided what to do next. He tried to use his power on them but there was a strong resistance. Luckily for the girls, although Axon had managed to manipulate Jonathan, for some reason he had no power over them. However, he was able to sweep them up in the air and they rose up inside the cloud.

Both the girls were terrified and all Geoffrey could hear were their screams. Elsa heard them too and immediately stopped climbing. Her loyalty to them was unquestionable, and although she was disobeying Geoffrey, she had no choice. She turned and raced down the rock with death defying speed. As she reached the path the cloud was already rising into the sky. She raced around in circles, barking and not knowing what to do. She heard Geoffrey call her and once again she started to scramble back up the rock, slipping backwards from time to time in her haste to get closer to Lizzie and Annie who were now rising above the Lion's Head.

Inside the cloud the girls were being tossed around as it swirled upwards. They were now high above Dovedale and they had never been so frightened in their whole lives. They could feel Axon's power trying to take them over.

'Stay strong, Annie,' Lizzie shouted to her sister. 'We must keep our minds focussed on each other. Don't give in to what you are feeling. It's bad Annie, you have to resist it.'

'I'm trying,' cried Annie, 'it's so hard.'

All of a sudden the cloud began to head downwards at a terrifying rate, sweeping past an enormous white cross. Without warning the girls found themselves tumbling the short distance to the ground. They landed with a bump on a grassy slope, just below the rocky summit of Thorpe Cloud. Axon swished and swirled above their heads and then in a flash he was gone, leaving them alone on top of the big hill with no idea of where they were.

'Are you alright, Annie?' asked Lizzie, trying to be very brave.

'I think so, but I was so scared. Oh, Lizzie, what are we going to do? Where are we?'

'I don't know,' said Lizzie despondently. 'But we'll find a way to get back to Geoffrey. Let's quickly have a look around and see if we can figure something out.'

Together they walked towards the big white cross that was towering in front of them. Without Geoffrey they felt quite insecure being so small, and the vastness of their surroundings was so daunting it was difficult not to panic and lose control. They slumped against the cross and looked at each other, neither knowing what to say. They felt desolate. Even Lizzie, who was normally so confident and self-assured, had no idea how they were going to get out of their desperate situation. The sound of voices broke their thoughts.

'Quick,' said Lizzie, 'run to the rocks. We have to hide.'

They ran as fast as they could and disappeared behind a rock just as the people arrived at the cross. In no time at all the two men had reached the summit.

Then it dawned on Lizzie where they were – Thorpe Cloud. Being so small made it difficult to get everything into perspective, but she knew she had to be right. They were certainly at the top of a big hill and the white cross was the extra bit of evidence to make her feel sure of her surroundings.

'Annie, they have a dog. Stay close to me.' Petrified, Annie snuggled up to her sister, praying that the dog would stay away. After a terrifying few moments when the two girls hardly dared to breath, it appeared that the dog was far too busy sniffing around below the summit. The two men sat down and leant against the rocks. They were both carrying small rucksacks on their backs and one of them took his off and got out a flask of coffee.

'It should be a nice stroll along the river to Milldale,' said one of the men.

'Yes, the views from here are certainly quite spectacular. I'm looking forward to climbing Ilam rock tomorrow, but I think you were right to suggest we look at it today. Everyone I know says it looks just like a finger pointing up towards the sky. It doesn't sound like it will be an easy climb.'

Lizzie's ears pricked up. The men would be walking right past the Lion's Head. As the men sat and enjoyed their drink, Lizzie had an idea.

She waited patiently for them as they chatted and relaxed, occasionally calling to the dog as he began to wander off. Once the man with the flask began to pack it away, Lizzie put her finger to her lips and signalled to Annie. Taking her firmly by the hand she almost dragged her onto the top of the other man's rucksack. It was placed so perfectly for them to climb on as he sat with it resting on the rock behind him. They were able to place themselves just behind the top of the bag, with their bodies close to the man's back.

Annie was totally unaware of what Lizzie was planning. Every time she opened her mouth to ask her Lizzie frowned, so she just had to trust that her sister knew what she was doing.

When the men started to walk again the girls had to hang on for dear life. The steep walk back down from Thorpe Cloud was particularly bumpy and these men were obviously very used to the outdoor life as they walked at a very fast pace. The colour was draining fast from both of the girls' faces. It was a bit like the feeling they had when they were on a fast rollercoaster, but this time they knew that if they loosened their grip they would fall.

Once they reached the path at the bottom the journey got a bit easier, but it didn't last long. Just as Lizzie was beginning to think it was safe to whisper to Annie the men began to climb some steps, causing the girls to shake around all over again. Soon they stopped and Lizzie and Annie found themselves peering over a steep precipice. The men were looking over the cliff at Lover's Leap. Lizzie felt sure they were going to fall over the edge. Annie let out a frightened squeal as she slid towards the top of the man's shoulder. Lizzie grabbed her ankle and tried to pull her back as she clung on with all her strength to the rucksack. She closed her eyes, as she couldn't bear to look. Thankfully, the men didn't hang around for long and they were soon striding along the path again.

As Lizzie looked at Annie she realised she was going to have to say something. The poor girl had no idea where she was and the whole experience was obviously affecting her badly. She looked almost green, and if Lizzie had not had such a firm grip on her arm, she could see that Annie could easily slip off and tumble to the ground.

'It's not much further Annie,' whispered Lizzie as softly as she could. 'They are walking right past the Lion's Head and when we get there we can slide down and jump off.'

'Are you sure?' asked Annie, perking up a bit and looking more hopeful.

'Quite sure, just hold on tight for a bit longer.' Annie smiled back at Lizzie. She could always rely on her sister to sort things out.

Chapter Seventeen

Back at the Lion's Head the tension was mounting. Geoffrey was beside himself with worry for the girls, not knowing where Axon had taken them or how he would ever find them again. As he looked down he caught sight of Elsa and he suddenly remembered Freddy and the boy. He knew he had to help them first before he could think what to do about Lizzie and Annie. Elsa had now almost reached the narrow ledge along the eye.

'Come on girl,' whispered Geoffrey. He carefully climbed out of the crevice and down under the Lion's eye so they were level with the opening. He patted Elsa, feeling so thankful that she had managed to get back to him.

'Geoffrey,' sighed Freddy full of relief. 'Am I glad to see you.'

Elsa came rushing forward and ran straight into the cave. Freddy took a quick step backwards, fear contorting his face.

'It's ok, Freddy,' reassured Geoffrey. 'She won't harm you. Axon has taken the girls and I don't know what we are going to do.'

'Girls?' asked Freddy curiously.

'Yes, twins. It's a long story, but if anything should happen to them, well I…'

'We'll find them, Geoffrey, but for now we have to get Jonathan safely away from here and us too.'

'You're right. Let's get this thing over with. Where is the boy?'

Freddy pointed over to where Jonathan was leaning against the wall. His face was ashen and there were beads of sweat on his forehead.

'He's sprained his ankle,' explained Freddy. 'This is not going to be easy.' At that moment Axon appeared at the opening facing Freddy, this time with Geoffrey by his side. Once again he tried to use his power and Freddy resisted by covering his eyes and ears. He mustered up all his strength and shouted at Axon.

'We just need a few more minutes and we will have the casket.'

The small amount of light was casting so many shadows in the cave that Elsa was becoming very nervous. She started barking randomly, racing around trying to make sense of what she was seeing. The cloud moved closer and swooped up into the cave. Freddy quickly signalled to Jonathan with a swift movement of his hand. Carefully, so as not to make a noise, Jonathan hopped outside the entrance. There was no time for hesitation, he knew he had to jump straight away, before Axon saw him.

With an almighty push off from his good foot he leapt out, arms outstretched to catch the branch of the nearest tree. As soon as he felt the soft leaves and the thin, twig-like branch in his hand, he knew it was no good. He heard the crack as the branch snapped under the weight of his swing and down he fell, brushing against the branches beneath him; none of them were strong enough to significantly break his fall. He could hear someone screaming in the distance. He was totally unaware that the scream was coming from him. As he hit the ground he felt his hand and arm bend underneath him and heard another snapping sound; then it all went black.

Geoffrey and Freddy heard the scream and stared at each other in horror. Axon was inside the cave circling over this strange creature that was darting about. Elsa, realising that the black cloud that had taken his precious girls away was back, directed her barking at that, masking the sound of Jonathan's scream. Geoffrey and Freddy edged away from the entrance.

'Elsa!' Geoffrey yelled at the top of his voice. The cloud swirled, but before Axon could work out what was happening, Elsa had bolted towards Geoffrey.

'Katia ngātahi' mumbled Freddy.

The eye began to slide shut as Elsa ran through into Geoffrey's waiting arms. Freddy couldn't bear to look; he just hoped that Axon wouldn't get there in time. As he heard the sound of rock upon rock, he slowly opened his eyes. He was stood on the narrow ledge in front of the Lion's eye with Geoffrey and Elsa beside him and no sign of the black wispy cloud.

'It's worked,' he hardly dared to mutter the words. He looked at Geoffrey as if for confirmation.

'We did it Freddy, we did it.' Geoffrey smiled and patted Freddy on the back. They both glanced down, remembering the penetrating scream they had heard moments earlier. They could just make out the body of Jonathan lying still on the ground.

Chapter Eighteen

Freddy led the way down the rock, carefully placing his feet in the crevices. Geoffrey followed on behind, whilst Elsa made her own way. She was quite an expert now.

Once they felt the path securely beneath them, Freddy and Geoffrey rushed over to Jonathan.

'Oh what have I done, what have I done,' wailed Freddy. 'It's all my fault and now Jonathan's dead.'

'He's not dead,' whispered Geoffrey, 'he's unconscious. He must have hit his head when he fell. We have to think of a way to get him help.' Geoffrey was studying Jonathan closely.

'He is lying on his arm in a very awkward way,' he said quietly. 'I wouldn't be surprised if it's broken, and that's probably not the only part of him that has been damaged having fallen all that way.'

'Someone's coming,' murmured Freddy with panic in his voice. 'Should we let them help him?'

'It's too risky,' said Geoffrey. 'Jonathan will want to know where you are when he comes round. He may start talking, we have to hide him.'

'How on earth are we going to be able to that?' sighed Freddy. 'He's far too heavy for us to move. We have to think of something quick.'

Geoffrey looked about him as if trying to see a solution. Then it came to him. Quickly, he put his hand on Jonathan.

'Nohinohi, nohinohi, nohinohi,' he chanted softly.

As Freddy watched on with amazement, Jonathan shrank to the size of a small Trignome.

'Wow! I've never seen that before. Where did you learn how to do it?'

'My grandfather,' replied Geoffrey. 'Now help me carry him to behind those trees. Be careful though, we don't know what he has broken. I'll take his head and shoulders if you can manage his legs.'

Carefully they carried Jonathan to the back of the clump of trees where they could not be seen from the path.

'Now, let's stay very still and quiet until these people pass by,' Geoffrey said calmly, although inside his little heart was beating so fast he felt sure it could be heard half way down the path.

Unfortunately for them it wasn't just people coming. Freddy recognised the sound of a dog bounding along before it reached them. They both tensed and didn't move a muscle.

It sounded like two men on a morning walk. As they got closer Geoffrey and Freddy could hardly breathe, they were so frightened. The sound of paws running towards them grew louder and then the barking started. They knew they were going to be in grave danger.

'Barney come here!' shouted one of the men.

To their relief Barney was a very obedient dog and went back to his owner straight away. Just as they thought their troubles were over they heard another, almost unrecognisable sound. It was a muffled sort of bark, followed by a squeal.

'Elsa!' whispered Geoffrey, shocked. In all their concern for Jonathan they had completely forgotten about the poor dog.

Geoffrey and Freddy were once more filled with anxiety and this time it wasn't for themselves or the children. Just as their worst fears were being realized, the voice of one of the men boomed out.

'Put that dirty thing down, Barney. Come here!'

'Oh, my goodness,' sighed Geoffrey. 'That dog must have found Elsa. I won't forgive myself if something has happened to her as well.'

They waited a few minutes until the men and dog were a safe distance away before rushing out towards the river, calling Elsa softly.

There she was, looking all the more like a drowned rat and shivering all over.

With a huge sense of relief and with Geoffrey holding on to her collar, they made their way back to the bushes. However, they didn't get very far. All of a sudden Elsa started barking excitedly and tugging like mad to try and get away from Geoffrey. She was so strong, Geoffrey inadvertently let her go and she darted straight along the path.

'Oh no!' sighed Geoffrey. 'Here we go again.' He was just about to rush after her when her barking changed to squeaking and two other little figures came into view.

'Lizzie, Annie,' Geoffrey yelled. He could hardly believe his eyes as he saw the two young girls running towards him with Elsa bobbing happily at their side. He held out his arms and embraced them both.

'You're safe! Oh, thank goodness. I've been so worried about you.' Geoffrey was so overcome with emotion that he sputtered out his words, just about making himself heard.

Lizzie and Annie smiled at him. Apart from looking a little dirty and dishevelled they were unhurt.

'It was terrifying,' panted Annie. 'That awful cloud took…' She paused as they all turned towards a faint groaning sound that was coming from the back of the trees.

'Jonathan!' cried Freddy as they all rushed towards him. He still lay motionless on the ground with his eyes closed.

'Oh, I don't believe it. It is our Jonathan and he looks like he is really hurt,' shrieked Lizzie, gazing at Geoffrey, her eyes full of concern.

Freddy knelt by his side.

'Jonathan, its Freddy, you are safe now. Can you hear me? Can you open your eyes?' He gently shook Jonathan's shoulders, but there was no response.

Freddy turned to look at the girls, completely at a loss as to what to do next. 'Look,' shouted Annie excitedly.

They turned to look at Jonathan, his eyes were open and he was trying to speak. 'Freddy, Freddy,' he whispered. 'Is he gone?'

'Yes, my dear boy, Axon is shut in the Lion's Head for ever.'

'My arm feels all funny,' Jonathan mumbled. 'My arm, my head, what happened?'

'You fell,' replied Freddy gently. 'You reached the tree when you jumped, but the branch just wasn't strong enough to hold you. Jonathan, we need to move you so we can see where you are hurt. We need to try and sit you up. OK?'

'Ok,' said Jonathan, 'I'll try.'

Freddy and Geoffrey put their hands carefully behind Jonathan's shoulders and gently raised his back off the ground.

'Aaah, my arm!' screamed Jonathan.

The girls rushed forward and it was clear that Jonathan's arm was indeed broken. He had fallen on it so awkwardly and you could tell it was distorted, despite the fact he had a coat on.

'Jonathan, it's me, Lizzie. Annie is here too. We need to

try and take your coat off,' she explained as she knelt beside him. 'It's going to hurt, but your arm will swell up very quickly and we need to try and strap it to your chest so it is a bit more comfortable.'

Geoffrey and Freddy looked doubtful. They were obviously not sure this was the right action to take.

'My friend broke her arm at school, that's how I know what to do,' Lizzie announced. 'Trust me, we can't leave him like this can we?'

Jonathan was looking at Lizzie and Annie in a very puzzled way, but he was in too much pain to start asking any questions.

'Just do it,' he said reluctantly.

Together they managed to remove Jonathan's coat with shouts and groans coming from the boy during the whole procedure.

'We need something to strap the arm to his chest,' said Annie. She thought for a moment. 'Geoffrey we could use your grass line, it's certainly strong enough and you can get some more for our journey home.'

'Of course,' said Geoffrey as he put his hand into his coat pocket and produced the line.

Lizzie did her very best to strap Jonathan's arm up as painlessly as possible, but there was no getting away from the fact that it had been a very uncomfortable experience. His pale face had turned almost ashen grey and his skin felt cold and clammy.

'Your ankle is swelling up too, said Lizzie. 'We need to take your trainer off.' She carefully untied the laces and with as gentle a tug as she could manage, the shoe came off. 'Try taking some deep breaths,' she said kindly, lightly placing

Jonathan's coat around his shoulders.

Jonathan had followed so many instructions over the past twenty-four hours, he did as he was told without thinking. Slowly, he began to feel a little better.

'I don't understand,' he began. 'How did you get here and how come we are the same size as Freddy?'

Lizzie and Annie laughed together.

'It's a long story,' said Annie. They proceeded to tell Jonathan how they had met Geoffrey and then flown here with him when he had heard the whistle message.

'That's just amazing,' said Jonathan, somewhat dazed. 'It's so good to see you both. I can hardly believe you are here.' There was so much to take in he could barely keep up with it all. 'Freddy, tell me what happened with Axon.'

'Oh, Elsa was the hero there.'

'Elsa! Is she here as well?' Jonathan sounded amazed. Lizzie called the still rather wet looking Elsa to her side.

'Here she is, looking a bit different to the last time you saw her.'

Jonathan held out his hand to let her sniff it and he patted her on the head. Elsa's tail wagged eagerly. She recognised Jonathan from the many hours they had spent together. He was always the one who never tired of throwing sticks into the river for her to fetch.

'Thank you for helping to save us up there,' he said gratefully. 'You did a good job.'

Elsa barked softly as if she had understood exactly what Jonathan had meant.

Chapter Nineteen

Geoffrey was still concerned to know what Axon had done with the girls. They told their story and their captive audience were all amazed how resourceful Lizzie had been in getting safely back to the Lion's Head.

As Lizzie and Annie continued to chat to Jonathan, trying to take his mind off the pain, Geoffrey and Freddy were also in deep discussion, wondering how they were going to best resolve the situation they were in.

'Jonathan's not going to be able to make it back to Ilam on his own, you know,' Freddy was saying to Geoffrey. 'In fact, he's not going to make it back there at all if I don't take him. He's got a sprained ankle that he can't put any weight on, a broken arm, and those are just the injuries we know of.'

'What do you suggest then?' asked Geoffrey, still conscious of the fact that he had to get the girls and Elsa safely back to Whernside and still be at Jasper's before they started to worry about where he was.

'You've made it a lot easier for me now you've made him small. He can fly with me back to his home. The only trouble is I have never heard of the enchantment you performed to make him that way and I don't know what to do to get him back to his right size.'

'That's no problem,' said Geoffrey laughing. 'It's simple; it's only a couple of words. Anyone can do it.' He proceeded to tell Freddy the enchantment and got him to repeat it several times, just to be sure he had it right. After all, they couldn't afford for anything else to go wrong. 'Problem solved then, and once I have the girls back on Whernside I can be on my way to Exmoor.'

'I can't thank you enough for what you did for me Geoffrey. Without you I dread to think what would have happened. Do you think Lizzie and Annie can keep our secret?'

'Yes, I'm as sure as I can be that they will,' replied Geoffrey confidently. 'And Jonathan?'

'Yes, absolutely. There's no way that little soul will be telling our story. You know we've both been so lucky to have met these children; it could have turned out to be so different.'

'You mean we could have all ended up dead with Axon back to his former self?'

'Well, that as well,' laughed Freddy.

They looked over to where the children were sitting. Jonathan had a little more colour to his cheeks now, but he was obviously trying hard not to show how much pain he was in. The odd little grimace and frown gave it away. He certainly was a brave lad.

'Time for us all to be on our way,' said Geoffrey. 'We've made up a grass line for each of us. Freddy is going to take you home, Jonathan.'

'But how?' asked Jonathan bemused.

'Now you are the same size as me, we can fly. It's not going to be that comfortable for you but it won't be for long, we haven't got far to go. There is one problem though.'

'What's that?' said Jonathan, concern in his voice. 'Your rucksack, it's too big for us to carry.'

'I can sort that out,' said Geoffrey. 'Where is it?'

Freddy pointed to the base of the tallest tree and sure enough there it was, just as Jonathan had left it the night before. Geoffrey went over, placed his hand on it and repeated the enchantment for the third time that day. Then he carried it over and gave it to Freddy.

'You are a very useful Trignome to have around, you know.' Freddy smiled at Geoffrey and they all laughed. Geoffrey passed him the new grass line he had prepared and they all helped to tie Jonathan and Freddy together. It wasn't easy to do it without hurting Jonathan, but they did their best.

'Thank you all so much,' Jonathan said once more. 'Will I ever see you again?' he asked Geoffrey.

'That may be difficult,' said Geoffrey.

'We'll see you in a few days though,' said Lizzie excitedly. 'We are staying at Aunty Sheila's and Uncle Alan's for a whole week, so we will have plenty of time to catch up on everything.'

'That will be great,' said Jonathan, pleased to think he would see the twins again so soon. 'Until then...' He patted Elsa and waved with his good hand to Geoffrey and the girls.

'Rere atu,' shouted Freddy. 'Thank you all.'

They lifted gently upwards and were soon a tiny speck in the sky.

'Now it's our turn,' said Geoffrey as he untangled the other grass line. The girls were still staring up into the sky, long after Jonathan and Freddy had disappeared out of sight. As Annie turned towards Geoffrey she saw he was watching them with a look of great fondness on his face. They had known each other for only a short while and yet they all felt such a close bond that united them beyond the passage of time. They had experienced such an array of emotions in that time, fear, joy, respect, anxiety and now sadness. Sadness, because none of them wanted to say goodbye. They didn't want to accept the realisation that they would never see each other again. Yet this was how it had to be. It would be reckless to risk another meeting, no matter where it was. Their worlds should never have crossed and for the safety of all Trignomes, they must never cross again. Nonetheless, it was still hard to accept.

'Come on, Elsa.' Geoffrey knew this was not going to get any easier so he had to get on with it. He passed the grass line around his waist and through Elsa's collar and under her tummy. Lizzie and Annie walked slowly and reluctantly towards him. They knew once they were back on Whernside the encounter would be over and they wanted to stay friends with Geoffrey for always.

Silently, Geoffrey attached the girls and soon they were bound together once more and ready to fly. With a heavy heart Geoffrey muttered the enchantment and they were off.

Chapter Twenty

It didn't take long for Freddy and Jonathan to reach Ilam. As Freddy had rightly said, it wasn't very far. When they neared the village they flew lower and Jonathan had a clear view of where they needed to go. Mrs Milson's cottage came into sight and Jonathan tapped Freddy on the arm and pointed down in that direction.

It was mid afternoon and Jonathan hoped Mrs Milson would be at home. He wondered how he would begin to explain how he had broken his arm and sprained his ankle. He had been so lucky really. Falling from that height could have been so much worse. He shuddered as he thought about it. Freddy looked up concerned, but Jonathan just smiled to reassure him.

They landed gently outside Mrs Milson's front door. Jonathan felt such a mixture of emotion; he could hardly hold back the tears. He was so relieved to be home safely. There were times over the last couple of days when he had thought he may never see this place again, or feel Mrs Milson's loving embrace. As he looked at Freddy he felt a sadness that made him feel hollow inside. This Trignome had taught him so much about family, loyalty, devotion, unselfishness and bravery. As Freddy gently untied the grass line Jonathan had no idea how he was going to be able to say goodbye. How could he lose this friendship when they had been through so much together? Some people go through their whole lives never experiencing what it's like to put your trust in someone and know they will not let you down. But that is exactly what Freddy and Jonathan had done. They had believed in one another and never doubted that they would be there for each other. The physical pain Jonathan was feeling paled into insignificance compared to the heartache he felt over losing Freddy.

'I have to change you back now,' Freddy mumbled quietly. He placed the rucksack by Jonathan's side.

'What are you going to do with the casket?' Jonathan asked. He wanted to know, of course, but he was also subconsciously trying to put off the inevitable. They were going to have to say goodbye.

'I think I need to smash the glass vial so it can never be used,' replied Freddy as he placed his hand instinctively inside his coat pocket. Immediately a rush of concern crossed his face and he started fumbling around, switching from one pocket to the other.

'What's wrong?' asked Jonathan.

'It's not there!' exclaimed Freddy, hardly able to believe the words he had just uttered. He checked his trouser pockets, just to be sure – nothing. The casket was gone!

'It must have fallen out when we were flying,' groaned Freddy. 'How could I be so foolish? I thought it was safe and now we have no idea where it is.'

'Don't worry, Freddy,' reassured Jonathan. 'Axon is locked up forever, he will never find it.'

'Yes, of course, you are right. It's just that I would have felt more secure about the whole thing if I had destroyed it. That's what I should have done as soon as we found it and not waited until after Axon had been trapped.'

'It's done now,' said Jonathan, with maturity beyond his

years. 'We had no idea what was going to happen when Axon confronted us. You couldn't have destroyed it before.'

Freddy looked deep into Jonathan's eyes. As he did so, Jonathan saw the pain in Freddy's. Freddy was feeling exactly the same as him. He didn't want their friendship to end either. However, Jonathan also understood that both Geoffrey and Freddy needed to keep their existence a secret and therefore meeting again would be far too risky.

'I'll never forget you Jonathan, or what you put yourself through to help me.' Freddy's voice caught in the back of his throat as he tried hard to fight back the tears.

'I will always be there for you Freddy,' sobbed Jonathan. 'I understand why we can't see each other again, but I want you to know that if ever you need me I will come. I remember what you said about your whistle and how a Trignome will always go to help another. Well, I will be like that with you. You do believe me don't you?'

'Yes, I believe you Jonathan, and thank you. You are such a special boy and there is a lady waiting in there who loves you very much. She's all you need you know, she is giving you the love of a mother and if you accept that, then your life will be a happier one. Maybe one day, when you are older, you will be able to find your real mum and then you can understand why she gave you up. From what you have told me she did a very brave and unselfish thing. She wanted more for you than she was able to give. That's not a bad thing Jonathan; sometimes when you love someone very much you have to give them up in order to do what is best.' Freddy was sure about that, as that was exactly what he was about to do. He placed his hand on Jonathan.

'Whakaora.'

Jonathan started to protest but it was too late. He found himself towering over Freddy. The pain in his arm was immense and as he looked down he realised it was no longer strapped to his chest. The grass line had snapped as he increased in size and it lay in pieces on the floor.

'Goodbye my very special friend, be happy,' said Freddy gently.

Before Jonathan had a chance to respond Freddy had mumbled his enchantment and was in the air. With tears streaming down his face Jonathan raised his hand to wave. He felt like his heart was going to break and he began to sob uncontrollably. Unable to summon up the strength to search for his key he stumbled to the front door and rang the bell.

The next few hours were a complete daze for Jonathan. After the first reaction from Mrs Milson of shock to find him on her doorstep in such a state, her love and concern took over and she decided to leave all the questioning until he was in a fit state to explain. She drove him straight to the hospital in Ashbourne, where he was X-rayed and then his arm was put in plaster and his ankle strapped up. There were no other obvious injuries apart from a few cuts and scrapes. Jonathan had managed to say that he had fallen out of a tree. He heard the doctor and nurse discussing whether to keep him in overnight or not. They asked him if he had knocked himself out and he said no, without giving it a second thought. He was totally unaware of the danger he might be putting himself in should he have any complications due to hitting his head. The hospital staff decided to keep him for another couple of hours, shining a torch into his eyes and getting him to grip one of their fingers every half an hour, when all he wanted to do was go home and sleep. Eventually, it was decided he was well enough to leave.

Once safely back in the cottage Mrs Milson put him gently to bed. The only question she asked was where Jack was.

'I didn't go to Jack's,' Jonathan murmured as he closed his eyes. 'I'm so sorry I lied, I will explain.' He was asleep within seconds and although all Mrs Milson wanted to do was find out exactly where Jonathan had been and what he had been up to, she could see he was completely exhausted. She sat on his bed and held his hand tight. Whatever had happened Jonathan would have a good reason for doing what he did, of that she was certain.

Several hours later Jonathan woke up, hungry and sore. It took him a few moments to take in his surroundings. The black and red striped curtains were drawn across the window, but it was still just about light enough for him to recognise where he was. The pine wardrobe and chest of drawers were a familiar sight, along with the poster on the wall of an old steam train Mr Milson had bought for him a few years before. He smiled; he was safe. His bedroom door was ajar and he could hear the faint sound of the television drifting up the stairs. He thought of Mrs Milson, waiting patiently for him to explain where he had been. It was time to go down and speak to her.

As he stepped out of bed he forgot about his sprained ankle and a shooting pain went up his leg as soon as he stood up. His arm was hurting too and his mind drifted to Freddy. He wondered if he was at home on Ecton Hill, or whether he would spend a few days with his family on Pen-y-ghent. The emptiness he had felt before swept over him and he had to fight back the tears as he thought of his dear friend. He took a deep breath and hobbled down the stairs.

Mrs Milson greeted him with a warm smile and after she had made him comfortable on the sofa, she went to the kitchen to collect his food she had prepared earlier. Once he had eaten she sat down next to him.

'In your own time Jonathan, tell me all about it.'

As Jonathan started to relate the events of the past two days Mrs Milson's face filled with horror. She wanted to ask him so many questions but she knew Jonathan just wanted to explain. He obviously had to miss out the bit about Freddy and that was extremely difficult. However, somehow he managed to tell a credible story about what had happened when he had left Thorpe Cloud. It wasn't that difficult really as he had spent all the time in Dovedale, so he just focussed on that.

'I am so sorry Mrs Milson,' and for the second time that day he started to sob. It all came out like a gushing river. His shoulders shook uncontrollably and he couldn't speak another word.

Mrs Milson leant forward and cradled him in her arms. At first she didn't speak. Jonathan felt her love for him flowing through her body into his. When his sobbing began to subside she spoke very gently.

'I understand Jonathan, I really do. I know how much it must hurt you not to have your real mum. I just want you to know that I love you as much as I would my own son. In my mind, you are the child Mr Milson and I always wanted and I wouldn't want to change anything about you. I think I have just taken all this for granted and perhaps not thought enough about how you were feeling. From now on we must be more open with each other and you must tell me if you are worried about something. I want to be here for you Jonathan – always.'

Jonathan lifted his head and wiped away his tears. He saw a touch of hurt in Mrs Milson's eyes and he knew it must have caused her pain to hear how unhappy he had been. It was time to put that right.

'I have learned so much about what life is really about since I left. I've thought through so many things and I now realise what I really want.'

Mrs Milson sighed. Jonathan hesitated, almost mistaking the resigned look on her face as possible rejection. Still, he was determined to put things right and after a lot of thought he was convinced this was the way forward to a happier and more settled life ahead.

'May I call you Mum?'

Mrs Milson visibly shot back with a jolt. This was so unexpected she couldn't speak.

'Of course, I understand if you'd rather…' Jonathan started.

'Oh, Jonathan, nothing in this world would make me happier. For a moment I thought you wanted to leave. Are you sure this is what you want?'

'Absolutely,' smiled Jonathan. 'You're the best mum anyone could ever wish for.'

Chapter Twenty-One

The girls had a very different journey back to Whernside than the one they had experienced earlier. Gone were the feelings of apprehension, excitement and awe. These were replaced with an overwhelming sadness. They reached the trig point far too quickly and this time their landing was very gentle. Geoffrey untied them all quickly and then they just stood there and looked at each other, no one wanting to say goodbye.

Elsa was the first to break the spell, recognising the familiar smells she sniffed around excitedly. She knew she had been there before.

'This is not going to be easy,' said Geoffrey solemnly. 'I don't think I have ever found it so hard to say goodbye.'

'No, we don't want to say goodbye either, but we know we have to,' said Lizzie.

'We will keep your secret forever, Geoffrey, you don't need to worry,' Annie babbled, taking in very quick breaths. Tears filled her eyes and she was obviously battling like mad to hold them in.

'I won't worry about that,' smiled Geoffrey. 'I just wish there was a way I could see you again, but there isn't. I'm so grateful that I literally bumped into you this morning. You have filled a gap in my heart and I will hold you there forever.'

'This doesn't really have to be goodbye forever,' deliberated Lizzie. 'Isn't there a way that if you ever needed us you could call on us and we would be there to help you. That way we can always feel that we may see you again. Something may happen one day when you need a human to be there too. It would be safer to fetch us rather than involve anyone new. The fewer people who know about Trignomes the better.'

Geoffrey marvelled at the wisdom of such a young child. He thought for a moment.

'Lizzie you may have a good point,' he paused, scratching his beard in a thoughtful sort of way. 'I've never been in a situation where I needed humans before, of course; that is, until today. I am not at all sure I would have been able to help Freddy so effectively if it had not been for Elsa and she wouldn't have been there if it had not been for you two.' He looked at the girls whose faces were fixed so intently on his.

'It certainly sounds like a good idea,' he continued. 'I just need to think of a way to make it work. The problem is, if I needed you then presumably I wouldn't be in a position to come and get you, so somehow you would have to come to me. How on earth could we make that possible?'

The girls were crestfallen. They knew that was impossible. 'Unless...'

'Unless what, Lizzie?' Annie asked excitedly.

'Geoffrey, you used an enchantment on us to make us smaller and it worked. Well, who's to say it won't work if we used it on ourselves?'

'No, that would be out of the question,' Geoffrey responded quickly. 'The enchantments are for Trignomes, and even if by some miracle it did work for you, you still would not be able to get to me. In order to fly you would need one of us.'

'I know another way,' Annie exclaimed. 'You can send messages to particular Trignomes right?'

'Yes,' replied Geoffrey, somewhat puzzled. 'We can send a message in a ball of light to any Trignome anywhere in the country. It travels very quickly so it's a very efficient way of communicating. Still, I don't see how this helps us with our problem.'

'It's the perfect solution,' chuckled Annie. 'We live in Taunton and you have a friend who lives in a trig point on Exmoor. That's a big area of course. What part does he live in?

'Selworthy Beacon, near Minehead,' responded Geoffrey immediately.

'Ideal,' said Annie. 'That's only about twenty-five miles away from us; it couldn't be better. If you need us you can send a message to him and then he can come and get us. It's simple. We explain where we live and to be extra safe, when he is nearby, he could just give a very short blast on his whistle, not to attract any Trignomes, but to alert Elsa. Dogs can hear very high-pitched sounds that humans can't, so it would work. When she starts to howl at seemingly nothing, like she does if there is an ambulance siren in the distance, we will know your friend is outside. What's his name?'

'Jasper,' said Geoffrey quietly, still trying to take in this ingenious idea.

'Wow! That's quite some plan Annie, well done you,' squealed Lizzie as she hugged her sister excitedly. They both turned to Geoffrey who was looking a little bemused.

'I suppose it would work,' he said hesitantly. 'I'd have to ask Jasper, of course; it's not without risk to him. However, it's not likely to happen very often if at all, so I'm sure he would be ok with it. Yes, that's the answer. So it's not really goodbye for good then?'

'No, not that we want you to be in trouble of course, but

if you ever need us for anything now you have a way of contacting us. That makes us feel so much better, doesn't it Lizzie.'

'Absolutely,' laughed Lizzie.

'That's settled then,' smiled Geoffrey. He gave the girls a fond hug and looked round to say goodbye to Elsa. Lizzie called her over and Geoffrey patted her head.

'You are quite some dog Elsa, thank you. It's time girls.' They nodded at Geoffrey; they were ready.

'Whakaora.'

Immediately Lizzie, Annie and Elsa were transformed back to their normal size. They found themselves gazing down at Geoffrey, who they could just about make out standing on the uneven ground by their feet.

Lizzie and Annie bent down and smiled at Geoffrey. 'Have a safe journey.'

'Until we meet again,' Geoffrey said softly. He moved a stone in the wall and took out his backpack. Turning to the girls he waved one last time to them. 'Rere atu.' Geoffrey rose up and headed off to Exmoor.

Elsa, Lizzie and Annie were all gazing towards the sky as the twins' parents reached the trig point. Geoffrey could hardly make them out now. What a strange day it had been so far and yet they had managed to overcome all the odds and were still left with the glimmer of hope that they may all meet up again one day.

Children, he thought, must be very special little people. At least, if the three he had met today were anything to go by, then he felt assured that the human race was in safe hands.

'Until we meet again.' Geoffrey smiled to himself as he rose higher in the sky.

Chapter Twenty-Two

As Jonathan lay in bed later that night, he felt contented, knowing that at last he could feel completely happy with his life. He had learned so much over the last few days and felt so many different emotions. It was hard to go to sleep with all the memories and thoughts going round in his head. However, he was also exhausted and soon his eyelids began to feel heavy. As he snuggled under his duvet, he slowly started to drift off to sleep.

'No, no!' Jonathan shouted as he woke up with a jolt. He wasn't sure how long he had been asleep, but a terrible thought had entered his head.

'The potion's lost! It's gone! Where is it? Will someone find it?'

Jonathan couldn't shake off a feeling of dread every time he thought about it. What if Axon could somehow get out of the cave and find it? Jonathan felt sure that Axon would find Freddy and who knows what he would do to him.

With a racing heart Jonathan began to envisage a raging Axon, back in his own body, planning his revenge on Freddy. He tried to think of how he could stop Axon getting hold of the potion.

'What can I do?' Jonathan wondered frantically. Then he remembered that Lizzie and Annie would be in Ilam in a few days. That was the answer, they could get together and the three of them would come up with a plan.

Drifting back off to sleep, Jonathan felt relaxed again. He convinced himself that there was nothing to worry about. Their plan would work and everything would turn out all right. That is, as long as they weren't too late…